MORE

of

THE MOSAIC

of

ALDERBURY

&

WHADDON

THE ALDERBURY & WHADDON
LOCAL HISTORY RESEARCH GROUP

First published by
Alderbury & Whaddon Local History Research Group
Hawthorns, Old Road, Alderbury, Wiltshire, United Kingdom.

Design by Frances Marr
Printed in Great Britain by Baskerville Press, Salisbury, Wiltshire.

ISBN 978-0-9538004-6-9

Acknowlegements

We are grateful for the assistance provided by the following:
Wiltshire Council for a Community Area Grant.
Salisbury & South Wiltshire Museum for permission to reproduce the painting of Miss Fort.
Wiltshire and Swindon Archives for permission to reproduce part of the will of James Langridge and the letterhead of A. Williams.
The Salvation Army International Heritage Centre for permission to reproduce the photos of the Fry Family.
Picture of Roy Pitman courtesy of Salisbury Newspapers (www.journalphotos.co.uk).
June Brind for providing drawings for the chapter on The Home Front.
Christine Marr for maps, line drawings and art direction.
Sue Wyatt for providing the update on the school.
Alderbury WI for photos from their archives.

Select Bibliography

Atkinson, R.F. *The Manors and Hundred of Alderbury*. Published by the author, Alderbury, 1995.

Briggs, Susan. *Keep Smiling Through: The Home Front 1939-45*. Book Club Associates, London, 1975.

Crocker, Emma. *The Home Front in Photographs: Life in Britain during the Second World War*. Sutton Publishing, Gloucester, 2004.

Gardiner, Juliet. *Wartime Britain 1939-45*. Headline Book Publishing, 2004.

Horn, Pamela. *The Victorian and Edwardian Schoolchild*. Alan Sutton, Gloucester, 1989

Pitman, Roy. *A Naturalist at Home*. Wiltshire Library & Museum Service, 1984.

Platts, A. *Wiltshire Schools: A Short History*. Published by the author, 1956

Alderbury & Whaddon Local History Research Goup

The Group was formed in 1998 by some enthusiastic amateur local historians determined to write a village history for the Millennium. The Group has continued with its research projects into the history of the parish, its buildings, institutions and people. It meets monthly for discussion and to report progress, and welcomes new members willing to contribute to its research aims.

The Group has a web-site www.alderbury.org.uk and has started an archive to collect items of information, family history, documents, letters, photographs, artefacts or anything connected with the parish. If anyone owns or knows of anything that might be of interest to the Group please contact any of the members.

Members 2011

Christine Marr (Chair)
Mary Hinchcliff (Secretary)
Brian Johnson (Treasurer)

Peter Hammond
Geoffrey Hatcher
Bernice Range

Margaret Smale
Ian Strong

Publications

Alderbury & Whaddon: A Millennium Mosaic of People Places and Progress (2000)
Alderbury War Memorials: In Freedom's Cause (2004)
Alderbury's Post Office (Looking Locally No. 1) (2005)
Inns & Alehouses of Alderbury & Whaddon (Looking Locally No. 2) (2006)
Saint Mary's Church, Alderbury (2007)
Brick & Tile Making in Alderbury (Looking Locally No. 3) (2008)

Contents

Foreword

In this new book entitled More of the Mosaic of Alderbury & Whaddon, we have continued our investigations into our local history, with many more photographs and an update of some of the changes that have occurred during the last decade. We hope it proves to be an introduction for our new readers as well as of interest to those of long-standing.

Evidence of the past is all around us, if we know where to look. As members of our local history research group, we each have particular interests that we like to explore, questions to which we seek the answers, information that we wish to share. How did evacuee children fare in wartime when they were plucked from their familiar city surroundings to live among strangers in a rural village like Alderbury? Or, where did people get supplies of water before it was available at the turn of a tap? And, as our new village school nears its 20th anniversary, how has education changed since the old Alderbury School opened its doors in 1838? We are pleased to be able to include some original field research too, as one of our younger members has investigated the earliest signs of habitation in our local area. These are just some of the topics that we hope will inform and intrigue.

As in our previous publications, we have striven to report as accurately as possible, untangling fact and legend and, when not mentioned in the text, we will keep our sources available on file. We thank all those who continue to encourage and support us by buying our books and sharing their memories. As a group fascinated by discovering our shared past, we hope to continue researching and publicising our findings. Already we have a number of projects nearing completion, including some excellent scripts by former residents, which will form a new series 'Village Voices'.

If you feel that you could contribute to our research, why not join us?

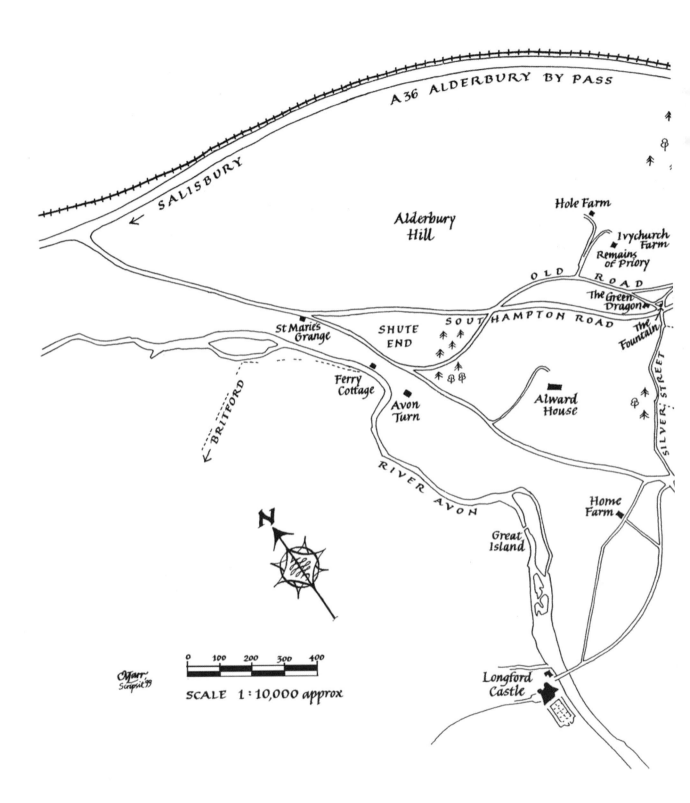

A36 ALDERBURY BY PASS

SALISBURY

Alderbury Hill

Hole Farm

Ivychurch Farm

Remains of Priory

OLD ROAD

The Green Dragon

SOUTHAMPTON ROAD

The Fountain

SILVER STREET

St Maries Grange

SHUTE END

BRITFORD

Ferry Cottage

Avon Turn

Alward House

RIVER AVON

Home Farm

Great Island

N

Longford Castle

O.Marr
Scripsit '93

0   100   200   300   400

SCALE   1:10,000 approx

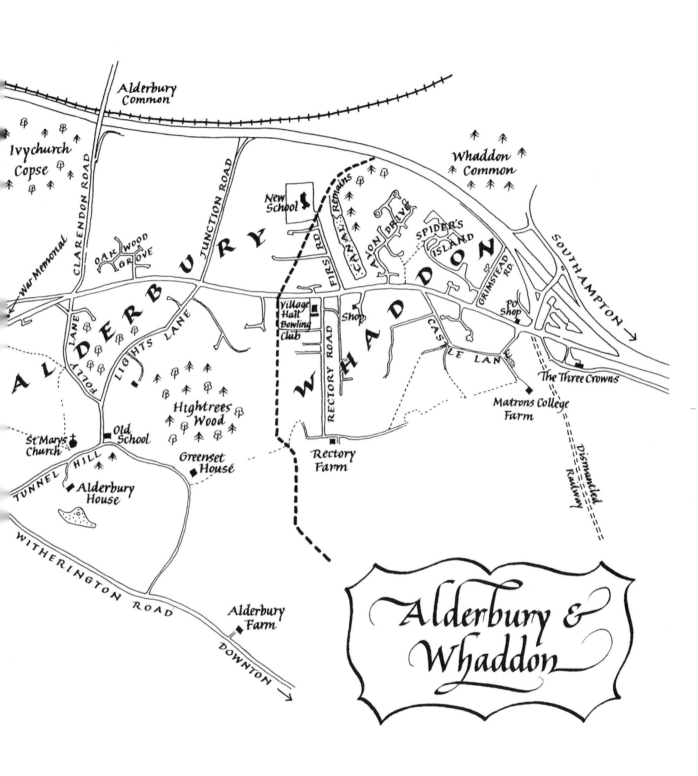

Alderbury & Whaddon

Out and About: A Village Exploration

In the 21st century the two villages of Alderbury and Whaddon have become a cohesive unit with a strong sense of community spirit. There are many properties that have stood for several hundreds of years and these are woven into the fabric of the modern village. In Alderbury, the dwellings along Old Road and Silver Street, together with those clustered around The Green, comprise some of the oldest. Whaddon's earliest settlements are located close to the Three Crowns and along Castle Lane. The farming community within the parish has shrunk with only a few working farms remaining. The village has been fortunate to retain its two pubs and village shops and recently has developed a successful business and commercial community in Whaddon.

ABOVE *The village sign and illustrated map on the green by Waleran Close.*

Some notable features

The Village Sign stands almost at the boundary between Alderbury and Whaddon and was erected in 2000 as a Millennium project. This decorative sign depicts the Fountain memorial with Alderbury Church between its pillars. A Victorian brick kiln representing the former Whaddon Brickworks, is flanked by the signs of the two inns: the Green Dragon and the Three Crowns. An old plough represents Agriculture, the former principal occupation of villagers. Bluebells symbolise the Clarendon Forest which centuries ago surrounded the village. Hidden in the picture are two amusing touches for children to discover. The illustrated Village Map nearby, was a community project celebrating the Queen's Jubilee in 2002.

The Fountain which stands on The Green was unveiled in 1902. It was commissioned by the parish to commemorate the Coronation of King Edward VII and in appreciation of the arrival of the first piped water supply to the village, courtesy of the Earl of Radnor of Longford Castle. Made of limestone and incorporating fragments from the ruins of Ivychurch Priory, it is both a memorial and a water trough. The War Memorial, also on The Green, is dedicated to those villagers who fell in two world wars. The Chilmark stone column was erected in 1919 on land donated by the Earl of Radnor. Nearby is a bench dedicated to the memory of William Foster GC, who was killed in a Home Guard exercise in 1942. The Victorian post-box on Shute End Road is the oldest in the village and bears the embossed letters VR.

Early milestone and remains

An early 19th century cast iron three sided pillar, at the Clarendon Road crossroads, has shields on two sides with the inscriptions 'TO SARUM 3 MILES' and 'TO SOUTHTON 19 MILES'. This is also the spot where legend has it that the village gallows stood. There is another milestone in Whaddon, near to the Post Office Stores, bearing the words 'SARUM 4$^1/_2$' and 'SOUTHTON 18'.

An interesting boundary post is situated on the east side of Shute End Road, facing the road up the hill. It was originally on the west side of the road, in the hedge of St Marie's Grange. It has 'listed building status' as a Grade 2, early 19th century Parish Boundary Post, cast iron of T form with panelled supporting post, and arms with the raised lettered inscription 'ALDERBURY/LAVERSTOCK'. It is one of only a few surviving parish boundary posts set up along the turnpike road. Interestingly, it refers to the Laverstock parish boundary, Clarendon did not exist as a parish until 1858. Clarendon was a 'Royal Liberty' without a parish church, this entitled residents to be buried in any of the adjoining parishes.

At the top of Silver Street, by the gate to Chuzzlewit, there is what is believed to be an Army Communications Junction Box. It comprises a brick-built structure approximately four feet wide by two feet six inches tall and ten inches deep. It has a metal door and is covered in ivy. It is a surviving artefact of the military presence in Alderbury from World War II. Remains of a milk stand can be found just inside the parish boundary, alongside the road at the entrance to Holt Farm, formerly known as Hole Farm. The long low platform built of breeze blocks, now covered in ivy, was originally topped with

ABOVE *Pillar, at the Clarendon Road crossroads and the milestone at Whaddon near the Post Office.*

The Pepperbox is a well-known feature on the southern approach to the village. It is a hexagonal red brick tower built in **1606** by Gyles Eyre. Otherwise known as Eyres Folly, it is situated on the chalk ridge overlooking the Avon Valley and originally had open arches at ground level. The two windows above each arch were blocked up in the 18th century when it became a notorious hideout for highwaymen waiting to attack the coaches toiling up Pepperbox Hill. It may originally have served as a lookout for hunting parties or been built as a rival to the towers at Longford Castle. During World War II the building was used as a lookout post by the Home Guard. An Observer Corps Bunker situated on the other side of the A36 from the Pepperbox, and hidden in the fields, was used as a monitoring station during the Cold War.

railway sleepers. It would have held 15 or 16 ten-gallon milk churns awaiting collection by the milk lorry. It was used until 1968, after which milk was collected by a tanker direct from the farm.

Around Silver Street

Silver Street is one of the original routes through the village and leads from the smithy down to the long ford on the River Avon where the castle is now situated, hence the name Longford Castle. The older properties on Silver Street originally belonged to the Longford Estate and were leased to estate workers. The majority of the old cottages date back to the 17th and 18th centuries and are under thatched roofs.

Silverman's Cottage was built in the 18th century and was originally two estate cottages. It has an original plank door with steps to the street. The cottage was refurbished and extended in approximately 2005. A local story concerns Mrs England, the village washer-woman who once lived there. Apparently, the Longford Estate Agent, who lived at Alward House, was not appreciative of his outlook across the fields to the lines of washing gently blowing in the breeze and so planted the stand of trees behind the Silver Street houses to improve his view.

Shoot End Farmhouse was a dairy farm before World War II, supplying the village with milk. It also served as the village Post Office for approximately ten years in the 1890s.

Old Timbers is a late 17th century detached estate cottage that was renovated around 1972 from two derelict cottages. A brick culvert behind the cottage, at the boundary line with the woods and running parallel to Silver

Street, was discovered by Mr Cochrane whilst digging in new fence posts.

Rose Cottage is also a late 17th century detached estate cottage renovated around 1950. The cottage was occupied for many years by the England family who farmed the adjacent land.

Rookwood, at the lower end of Silver Street, is a detached house renovated from three former estate cottages. The owners indicate the presence in the house of a well, dated around 1500. The house was partly thatched until the 1980s.

Wisteria Cottage dates from the 19th century and was formerly the home of the Eyres family, local builders with a yard on the opposite side of the street.

Old Road and Clarendon Road

Several interesting houses are grouped near the Green Dragon Inn. *Jasmine Cottage*, a picture perfect thatched cottage on The Green, formerly belonged to the Longford Estate and was known as Rose Cottage. A previous owner believed that it was the home of the estate river keepers and is over 200 years old. The inner lining of the thatched roof still has its original hazel branch construction. In 1852 George Dowty lived in the house and it was used for religious meetings of the Primitive Methodists before their chapel opened in Whaddon in 1884.

LEFT *Jasmine Cotttage on The Green.*

13

Lake House is a mid 18th century detached house. This former estate house, sold to a Mr Nathaniel Lane in May 1809, was inherited by his son, Charles Lane Lake, in 1842.

Fountain View is a detached house opposite the War Memorial, which was built in 1927 by the retired postmaster, Mr Northeast. His son, Will Northeast, says that the land was purchased from the Salisbury horse dealer, Mr Penny, who kept his horses in the adjoining sheds.

Ye Olde Post Office Cottage is another very pretty double fronted thatched cottage that served as the village Post Office until 1956. The last postmaster was Mr Maidment who was an ARP warden during World War II and when the War Memorial was being dedicated after the war, he interrupted the service by playing the Last Post on his trumpet from the cottage doorway. During renovations in the 1950s, its cob walls were refronted.

Cherry Tree Cottage on the corner of Old Road is an 18th century former estate cottage that originally would have been thatched. It is not known when the thatch was removed but when the property was sold in 1937, it had a slate roof. A map of 1820 shows a windmill in the field behind the cottage, but no trace of it remains.

Long Close, on the north side of Clarendon Road, is a small house set into the bank and built by John Belstone, a local bricklayer, who was born in Alderbury in 1793. He was a ratepayer, married twice, had three children, and lived in the house for over 40 years. There is a reproduction plaque on the front of the house 'JB 1830' with the original

built into a wall at the rear of the property. The largely rebuilt house retains most of its original layout.

Hillside House, also on Clarendon Road was the home of the Thesiger family in the 1950s and the first recorded Roman Catholic Mass in Alderbury was held here in 1955.

Folly Lane

High Street leads off Folly Lane and is a picturesque row of cottages and old houses, overlooking allotments. It once incorporated a village shop and the Goose Inn. Progressing down Folly Lane, *Holly Tree Cottage* was renovated and extended in the 1980s and the windows from the demolished adjacent Wesleyan Methodist Chapel were incorporated in the design to present a charming façade.

Totterdown Cottage is late 18th century and part thatched. It was the former home of Mr Hibberd, a carrier, who ran a horse and cart service into Salisbury on market days. He would leave Alderbury at 10am, returning at 4pm, charging adults 3d and children 1d for the return fare. The service started in the late 1800s and ran until 1921 when a bus service was introduced.

Yew Tree Cottage was the home of the village nurse before the NHS was introduced and she was allowed to live there rent-free by the Longford Estate. It is a 19th century well-designed example of an estate cottage but previous owners believed that the presence of wattle and daub walls in the central core indicates that at least part of the building is older. It was formerly known as Ivy Cottage and has been privately owned since 1976 when it

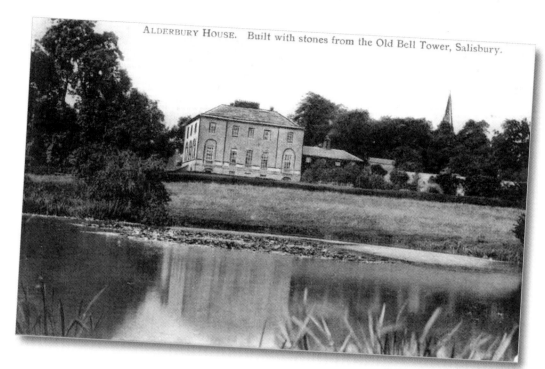

ALDERBURY HOUSE. Built with stones from the Old Bell Tower, Salisbury.

LEFT

Old post card of Alderbury House and lake.

was substantially renovated. A local legend records a cook setting fire to the chimney there. Numbers *5, 6,* and *7 School Hill* are pretty 17th century estate thatched cottages with 1950s renovations. It is thought that the village chimney sweep, Yebbie Belstone, lived in one of the houses in the 1920s.

Around the Parish Church

Several substantial houses are located near St Mary's Church. *Alderbury House* was built for George Yalden Fort in 1791 on the site of the earlier family house which was incorporated into the service wing. The contractors, Henry Ford of Wilton, purchased stone from the demolished medieval Bell Tower of Salisbury Cathedral for the house. The belfry was pulled down as part of James Wyatt's restoration of Salisbury Cathedral circa 1789-92. Recent research by a team of American architects links the house to the London firm of Sir Robert Taylor and Samuel Pepys Cockerell. From 1788-91 their chief draughtsman was Benjamin Latrobe who later became America's First Architect. Drawings of Alderbury House were found in the 'English Notebook' in the Latrobe archive in Washington. Latrobe was hired by United States President, Thomas Jefferson in 1803 and is famous for his designs for the White House porticos, the central portions of the United States Capitol Building, and for the design of the first Roman Catholic Cathedral in the USA. Alderbury House stands in landscaped parkland that includes a lake constructed as part of the Salisbury and Southampton Canal. The American researchers report that it is the least altered and most completely preserved of all Latrobe's surviving houses in England or America. Local residents

15

ABOVE *Court House near St Mary's Church.*

say the house was used during World War II as Officers Quarters.

Alderbury House Lodge, a mid 19th century cottage is of importance due to its connection with Alderbury House. Several courses of 18th century brickwork along the base of the north and west walls suggest evidence of an earlier building.

Greensett House, formerly known as The Vicarage, is a substantial red brick house. There is a date on the S.E. gable of 1851. Canon Hutchings lived there from 1865-74 and he had an observatory built in the garden.

Court House is a part brick and timber framed building standing to the east of St Mary's Church. The present house is thought to have been rebuilt in the early 18th century but has a 16th century rear wing. It is first mentioned in the 1649 survey as Alderbury Rectory (not a vicarage). In the 1814 Parish Survey it was listed as the village poor house and at a meeting of the Board of Guardians of the Alderbury Union in 1835 *'the presence of a poor house next to the church'* was noted. In the 1851 Census it is listed as The Parsonage and accommodated three families. We know from the census that in 1861 Abraham Lewis, his wife and three brothers, moved there from Silver Street. He was tailor to the Earl of Radnor making livery and uniforms. Between 1836-63 they had 21 children. Zoe Long, who lived there with her parents until 1930, relates that in 1926 the house was called The Old Rectory. It was divided into two residences and belonged to Lord Radnor. The Newson family lived in the part nearer the church; George Newson was in charge of the kitchen garden at Longford Castle and also played in the Alderbury Band. The house subsequently became known as Church House and there are indications that it probably remained subdivided until 1973 when it was sold into private ownership having been advertised in Country Life magazine as a 'Queen Anne Country House' and renamed Court House by the Estate Agents. The house was substantially refurbished in 2006.

The Old School House, on School Hill, was formerly the village school, founded by the Earl of Radnor in 1838. It passed into private hands in 1993. It is a brick and timbered medieval hall house of the late 15th century. The interior, which was originally open to the roof, was floored over in the 17th century. According to an estate survey of 1765, the site was owned by George Fort and comprised a farmhouse with land, yards and barns leased to George Grey. Early in the 19th century, the site was acquired by the Earl of Radnor and the list of successive leaseholders includes the names of Windsor, Lawrence, Tanner and Bungay.

High Trees House was occupied by the army in World War II. Mrs Greenwood lived there between the war years and is remembered locally for '*the large hats she wore to church, the brims of which were laden with fruit and flowers*'.

A look around Whaddon

Whaddon has several modern housing developments while still retaining dwellings of character and history. *Castle Hill House*, in Castle Lane, is a substantial, early 19th century, three-story detached house with an internal well. Tom Dowty lived there as a boy.

The Old Cottage is a detached, early 18th century former estate cottage with deeds indicating private ownership from 1914. An 18th century barn at the rear of the property is large enough to have possibly housed a horse and cart or carriage and this leads the owner to believe that the cottage may have been occupied by a substantial tradesman.

TOP *The pub sign for the The Green Dragon.*

ABOVE *The pub sign for The Three Crowns.*

17

Rose Cottage, situated at the end of Castle Lane, opposite the Post Office, is early 19th century. It adjoins what used to be the old Whaddon Smithy. (It was not the site of a hostelry called The Queen's Head, as previously thought.)

Ladies Cottages, formerly known as Ball Cottage, has been modernised recently, but was also previously known by local people as The Barracks, perhaps meaning '*a building of plain or dreary appearance*'.

Tetherings was formerly a pair of semi-detached cottages built in 1826. It was owned leasehold by George Light and both cottages were let - one to Thomas Hibbard and the other to James Williams.

Canal House, on Southampton Road, was built in 1870 on the site of a former dwelling. One of the village milkmen lived there and probably also farmed the land around.

The Old Police Station was commissioned by Wiltshire Constabulary as the area Police Station and the Police Sergeant lived there. Constables from the surrounding area were required to attend meetings there every Friday morning. It was decommissioned around 1982.

Crossfields was the home of Ralph Tanner, the local brickmaker.

Rectory Farm is a square fronted house dating to the early 1800s. The farm acquired its name after the 1809 Enclosure Award and indicates an association with Alderbury Rectory Manor. There is a listed 18th century barn at the farmyard, currently used as a cowshed.

Matrons College Farmhouse is listed as late 17th century with several later additions. There are two carved stone heads on the west aspect, one male and one female. They are thought to be medieval and may have come from Ivychurch Priory or Whaddon Church. Formerly known as Charity Farm, it was endowed by the Bishop of Salisbury to provide an income for clergy widows living in Matrons College in Salisbury Cathedral Close. It was sold in the 1980s and today the house is in private ownership and the land incorporated into Alderbury Farm.

The Three Crowns Inn, a traditional hostelry is described fully in a separate booklet.

Shute End

Another cluster of interesting dwellings lies just inside the parish boundary at Shute End. *Avon Turn* is a rectangular detached mid 18th century house standing in landscaped gardens on the banks of the River Avon. It was formerly called Alderbury Cottage and from 1797-1843 was the home of the Geddes family who were to become parents and grandparents to an extended family of eminent artists and authors, the most famous being Wilkie Collins. The house was fully renovated in the late 1960s. Later, it became the home of the Dowager Countess of Radnor.

Ferry Cottage, also near the river, was the home of the Hazel family who ran a ferry across the Avon to Britford. The W.I. history of Alderbury records '*old Mrs Hazel recalled taking Charles Dickens across in the ferry*'.

Alward House stands between Shute End and the church. The history of the house is not well documented but during the years that included World War I, it was occupied by Mr Ralph Macan, agent to Lord Radnor and the Longford Estate. He organised the local

Red Cross volunteer force supporting the military hospital at Longford Castle while his wife knitted mittens for the troops and organised parcels. Villagers remember that the house was requisitioned by the military during World War II and there was a camp of army Nissen huts in the nearby woods. A former Alward House employee gives a clue to its function during the post World War II period. Wiltshire Agricultural Executive Committee ran it as a hostel for 35 volunteer war refugee workers, mainly from Poland, Hungary and Yugoslavia, who were hired out to local farmers in the 1950s. An important part of the warden's job was to liaise with the local police with regards to movements under the Alien Registration Act. When the hostel eventually closed many of the refugees found permanent work in the area.

St Marie's Grange, just over the parish boundary, is a house built by the famous Victorian architect, Augustus Pugin (1812-1852). He purchased the plot of land in 1835 and designed and built the house as a vision of Gothic domestic architecture, noting in his diary *'it is the only modern building that is compleat in every part in the ancient style'*. The plot of land sloped sharply down to the river so the house was built close to the road to take advantage of views across the river to Salisbury Cathedral in one direction, and Longford Castle in the other. The original design of the house, with steep roofs, turret and towers, was small despite its grand pretensions. Pugin and his second wife, Louisa, lived in the house for two years and their second child, a girl, was born there. However, his wife *'didn't like the Salisbury air'* The new owners added to the internal accommodation and changed the layout by adding a spacious entrance hall, new staircase and bell tower.

Belmont House stands close by on the Southampton Road. It was built in the mid 19th century for John Staples, a wine merchant. Local stories suggest some of his wines were delivered by boat on the River Avon that flows along the boundary of the property. In the 1880s, Mr Staples tried to make a waterfall in the river with stones brought from Ivychurch Priory ruins. In 1954, a local builder dug out the river at the same spot and recovered several artefacts including a drum-shaped stone, with a hole through the middle, and the keystone of a 14th century arch. The converted former stables of the house are now a separate dwelling further along the main road, which is called *Clarendon Grange*.

Recent modern developments

In Alderbury, Silver Wood is a small cluster of detached houses, opposite the tennis courts, built by Downton Village Homes in 1996 on the site of the former wood yard. It involved the demolition of the former Girl Guide hut and a telephone exchange.

During World War II, American Forces occupied the site for servicing their military vehicles prior to joining the D-Day invasion force. Children at the time, remember that the GIs slept in glider cases stacked on top of each other. Will Northeast used to bring them bread from Occomore's bakery where he worked.

Avon Drive is a development of over 250 houses on the former Whaddon Common, built by the firm of George Wimpey in the late 1970s and early 1980s. Oakwood Grove consists of 50 houses built in the 1980s by Dunnings. In

19

Whaddon, Pepperbox Rise was developed in the 1990s on the site of Yeates' Garage and The Sandringhams was also built in the 1990s on the site of the old sandpit.

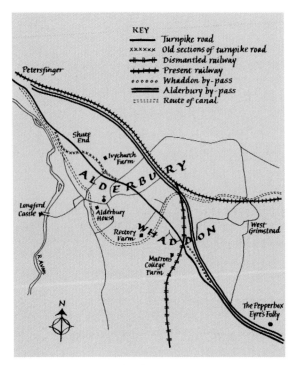

ABOVE *The proposed route the canal was to take is shown by the dotted line.*

The Old Canal

The mid-late 18th century was a time of rapid industrial expansion which required improved transport links. Before the railways, the cheapest way to move goods was by water. In 1795, an Act of Parliament was passed allowing the Southampton to Salisbury Navigation Company to build a canal from the eastern side of Southampton to the Andover Canal at Redbridge, and from Kimbridge through Alderbury, to Salisbury. The project was beset by financial difficulties and poor progress from the outset, and a major effort to raise funds to complete the work failed. By 1805, the canal was in decline. The gradual decay of lock gates meant that upper reaches of the Salisbury arm of the canal became stagnant, then dry, while the remainder reverted to a small stream. It has long been a myth in the village that the canal failed when it reached Alderbury because it hit sand and would not hold water. There is no evidence to support this, as the reason for the failure of the venture was that the project simply ran out of funds.

The most obvious remnant of the ill-fated canal remaining today can be seen alongside Firs Road in Alderbury. Known locally as the "old canal", this has the appearance of a small lake, with old, water-logged tree stumps poking from the surface. This was not the canal basin, which was to be nearer to Salisbury. In reality, the canal ran along the bottom of this shallow depression alongside Firs Road; the small artificial lake was created when the area was dammed with the spoil excavated during the building of the Alderbury bypass in the 1970s.

Traces of the route of the old canal itself can still be seen elsewhere in the parish, sometimes as a shallow cutting or through a line of hedgerow where it was not ploughed out. There was also a reservoir lake in Clarendon Park to supply the summit, fed by a small channel via Pope's Bottom and Walden Farm. This lake, which is now ornamental, was developed over the years by the landowner as a wildlife garden. The area below the church is one of the most easily accessible and recognizable of the dry sections to find. The line crossed under the road in a short tunnel close to the present 30 mph sign, the tunnel, which was filled in long ago, led to a man-made lake in the grounds of Alderbury House which still survives. The line of the canal after it leaves the grounds of Alderbury House as far as Shute End, is shown on a map dated 1824. From the point where it left Tunnel Hill, the route went north across the field below the church, following the double line of trees. It then turned north-west to cross the bottom of Silver Street and ran along Shute End Road to the edge of the site subsequently used by Pugin to build St Marie's Grange. The line on the map is dotted, suggesting that at this time, much of stretch of the proposed canal had not been built.

Road Names – is Yours Mentioned?

Modern road-names are often picked by developers, sometimes consulting the parish council, sometimes not. An example of the latter is **The Sandringhams**, which has faint

ABOVE *The 'old canal' near Firs Road.*

echoes of the major sandpit that stood on this site but probably, has more to do with the sales image the developer wished for this estate. Councillors look with favour on names that commemorate the history of the area; for example **Waleran Close** named after the Norman huntsman to whom William the Conqueror gave the manor of Whaddon. **Eyres Drive** is named after Giles Eyre who built the folly known affectionately to villagers as 'The Pepperbox'. This landmark is actually just over the parish boundary in Whiteparish but is more visible to Alderbury residents. It also gives its name to **Pepperbox Rise**.

    Windwhistle Way, off Avon Drive, took its name from Windwhistle Farm, which used to stand on Windwhistle Lane, the exposed road leading from Pepperbox Hill to West Grimstead. Nearby **Priory Close** is a reference to Ivychurch Priory, an important part of Alderbury's history. **Windmill Close** gets its name from Whaddon Windmill, which stood on that site. It has been said that **Spiders Island** took its name from a symbol for that windmill which, on a map of 1809, resembled a spider. Certainly on subsequent maps Spiders Island was shown as the name for that area. **Kiln Close** stands on part of the site of the former Whaddon Brickworks.

21

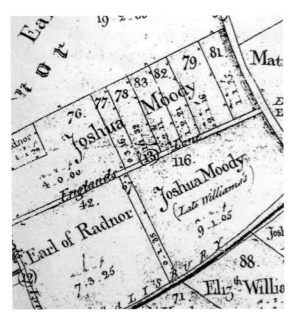

ABOVE *Part of the 'Enclosures Award' 1809 showing Rectory Road as Englands Lane.*

Junction Road led to the railway's Alderbury Junction. **Tunnel Hill**, on the other hand, is associated with the canal tunnel that led from the lake in the grounds of Alderbury House and under the road. Older residents remember a culvert or tunnel under the road, emerging by the line of trees in the field below the church. The south side of **Canal Lane** backs on to the vestiges of that canal, the ill-fated Salisbury and Southampton Canal. **Canalside**, off Avon Drive, also takes its name from it.

Names are not always constant over the years. **Rectory Road**, which leads to Rectory Farm, is shown on the 1809 Enclosure Map as Englands Lane. How the family of that name who lived there in the latter part of the twentieth century would have loved that! The lane across the bottom, now part of Rectory Road, was shown on that map as Wards Lane. Again, **Castle Lane** was not always so named;

at one time it was Whaddon Lane and prior to that only the small section east from Ladies Cottages was called Castle Lane. The other section from the present Post Office was called Bungays Lane (a local family for many years). It was shown on the 1809 map as turning left at Ladies Cottages, past The Tetherings and over the field to the cottage now known as Crossfields and a group of cottages which no longer exist. Castle Hill was so named in a 1790 document and, as the highest point in the hamlet of Whaddon, it is possible that in Norman times there could have been an earthen castle motte here.

Some of the older names are of interest. Shute End (or Shoot End as it has sometimes been known in the past) is derived from the Old English 'sceat', a corner, being a projecting corner of the parish. It is generally agreed that **Silver Street** comes from 'silva' or 'sylva' the Latin word for a wood. We do not know why **Folly Lane** is so called but many believe it may be derived from the Norman French 'folie', meaning foliage. **Old Road** was the original main road from Salisbury, which wound its way up from Shute End Road before the new turnpike road took the more direct route.

Opinions differ on the origins of **Lights Lane**. There are those who think it came from the Medieval English 'liche', a body, being the route taken by those carrying bodies to the church for burial. Others suggest it gets its name from the Light family who have been in the area for hundreds of years. It was certainly spelled 'Lits Lane' in 1640 when, at the Quarter Sessions, it was presented as being out of repair: *'Church Way leading from Whadon to Allderbury Church in a place called Lits Lane, not sufficient'*.

In the Beginning

Ten Thousand Years of Human Activity

Alderbury and Whaddon did not exist as villages in the landscape, as we know them today, until probably at some point during the Saxon period. There are Saxon earthworks to the north of Alderbury and it is very likely that the church in Alderbury was built on the site of a former Saxon church. However, the archaeology would indicate that there has been human activity in the parish since the ice sheets retreated at the end of the last ice age, some 10,000 years ago. Part of the reason for this may be due to its location.

The natural route over the downs to the south of the villages is along the ridge which rises up to Witherington Down on which the A36 was constructed. It may be a coincidence but the majority of the early finds have been found along this ridge, which would suggest that it may have been a main route from pre-history. Possibly because the valleys to either side of the ridge were either too wooded or too marshy to cross. From the ridge there are commanding views over the River Avon to the west and the Dun valley to the east. Also the chalk downland on which the parish is situated is fertile and easily drained making it ideal for both arable farming and animal husbandry.

The Mesolithic and Neolithic Period 9,500 BC to 2,300 BC

The oldest finds from within the parish date from the Mesolithic period when it is generally thought that people were hunter gatherers living nomadic life styles, usually following game. Several flint tools have been found relating to this period within the village which most probably represent the material remains of hunter gatherer family groups who were making their way along the Avon valley.

The Neolithic period followed the Mesolithic and dates from around 4,000 BC. It is thought that by this period people had begun to settle and farm the land. There have been several flint finds dating from this period within the parish. The most significant being a varied collection of flints which was found near Pepperbox Hill. This find may indicate a site where flint knapping had taken place and therefore possibly the site of a settlement, occupied by a small farming community.

The small farming communities of the Neolithic were probably no more than extended families. Although they were more settled than the people of the Mesolithic period they still moved location from time to time, probably once the land on which they were farming had become exhausted. Not until the early Bronze Age period did the small farming communities became permanently settled once they had learned how to maintain the fertility of the land.

The Bronze Age 2,300 BC to 700 BC

During the Bronze Age it is likely that the River Avon which flows north/south to the west of Alderbury would have been an important route. It is worth noting that the River Avon also flows

23

RIGHT *Bronze Age burial sites and ancient settlement sites found near Alderbury.*

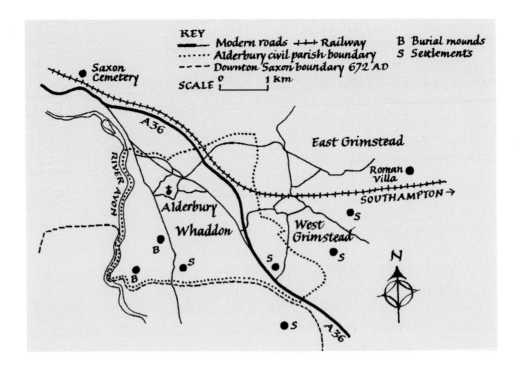

close to Stonehenge. Recent excavations at Stonehenge would suggest that the river linked the living world at Durrington Walls (where a large pre-historic settlement has been discovered) with the world of the dead at Stonehenge. The dead were ceremoniously brought along the river from Durrington Walls to Stonehenge to be either cremated or interred in a burial mound often referred to as a barrow or tumulus. It was during the Neolithic and Early Bronze Age that burial mounds became the principle funerary monuments in the landscape.

From a review of the aerial photographs of the parish it is probable that there are at least two burial mound groupings located adjacent to the River Avon, each consisting of at least five circular barrows or tumuli. Both groupings were built on high points adjacent to the river presumably to protect them from flooding but close enough to enable the passage of the deceased from the world of the living to the world of the dead.

The existence of burial mounds in Alderbury is the first tangible evidence to suggest that there was permanent settlement within the parish from at least the Early Bronze Age, as it is unlikely that the burial mounds would have been constructed without settlement in close proximity.

Early Settlement

The local aerial photographs combined with field walking evidence suggest that there were five small settlement sites within the locality, each separated by about two miles. This pattern of small, scattered, sites is typical of settlement patterns found elsewhere on chalk downland. As such, the local community during this period probably comprised small family groupings, each farming a smallholding.

One of the five settlements, is adjacent to Windwhistle Lane and the A36. This site (hereafter referred to as Windwhistle) has been extensively researched by one of our members and is probably typical of the other four settlement sites within the locality. It was one of a possible pair of enclosures situated just off the ridge up to Witherington Down which carries the current A36.

The earliest find from Windwhistle, a sarsen saddle quern, has been dated to the Late Bronze Age. In addition, another quern stone was found on the site which unfortunately was undateable. It was likely to belong to either the Bronze Age or Iron Age as it predates rotary querns. The presence of quern stones within the site would suggest that arable farming and food processing was taking place. Several pottery sherds from the Iron Age and Roman period were also found there. This evidence suggests that the Windwhistle site dates from the Late Bronze Age and continues throughout the Iron Age and Roman periods. The primary function of the site throughout these periods was likely to be agricultural in nature.

Although it is difficult to prove, comparison with similar chalk downland Iron Age sites would suggest that the settlement may have contained between 40 to 70 individuals during the Iron Age period.

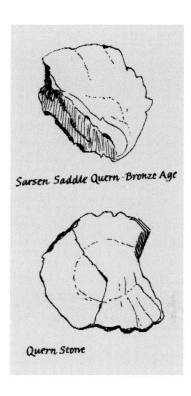

Sarsen Saddle Quern - Bronze Age

Quern Stone

The earliest find from Windwhistle, a sarsen saddle quern, has been dated to the Late Bronze Age. The presence of quern stones within the site would suggest that arable farming and food processing was already taking place.

The Iron Age 700 BC to 43 AD

The five settlement sites continued throughout the Iron Age. Typically settlement during the Iron Age, as in the prior period, took the form of several roundhouses situated within a ditched enclosure. Sometimes the enclosure was palisaded. The site at Windwhistle conforms to this layout and it was also most likely palisaded for a period.

The evidence from the aerial photographs shows that by this period the settlements were located within an extensive 'celtic' field system, suggesting a settled organised landscape and one that was being farmed. Grain was often stored in pits which were dug into the chalk. These pits could be quite deep, up to

Post Conquest pottery sherd
1st C. AD

25

about six foot in depth and four foot across although the size and shape varied. Once emptied of food they tended to fill up with general domestic waste and it is from these pits that many of the finds from an Iron Age site are discovered. Although no excavations have been undertaken at the Windwhistle site, pits have been excavated at similar contemporary Iron Age sites. The contents of these are likely to be similar to those at Windwhistle, which contained 112 pits, although they are unlikely to all have been contemporary, given the life span of the site. At the excavated Iron Age settlement at Little Woodbury (located near Salisbury Hospital) the animal remains from the pits indicated the presence of small ox, small sheep, small horse, pig and dog. As well as animal husbandry and arable farming there is also possible evidence of industry having been carried out on the site at Windwhistle. A piece of slag was found which would indicate the presence of smelting, although it is not possible to determine the period to which it relates.

With permanent settlement, such as at Windwhistle, trading links would begin to be established between the coast and the interior, primarily along the waterways. Situated near the mouth of the River Avon is Hengistbury Head where it is known that there was a large Iron Age settlement which had trading links to the continent. It is likely that trade links would have extended from Hengistbury Head back into the interior along the river, giving the settlement at Windwhistle and elsewhere on both sides of the river, access to trading links on the continent.

It is probable that the River Avon marked the boundary between two tribes. It is from this period that the various tribes that made up Britain are known. The evidence is based on Roman classical references, regional ceramic traditions, and coins, which began to be minted and circulated in the Late Iron Age.

To the east of the river was the territory of the Atrebates in which Alderbury is situated and to the west was the territory of the Durotriges. The hillfort at Clearbury Ring, in the territory of the Durotriges, would have been clearly visible from Windwhistle with the banks forming a white chalk scar, on top of Clearbury Down. No excavations have been undertaken at Clearbury, but given its form, it is likely to be Iron Age in date. Although it has been described as a hillfort it was unlikely that its primary purpose was as a defensive enclosure. A more practical purpose may well have been to kraal cattle to stop them being rustled. This may also be why some settlement enclosures were ditched and palisaded, as at Windwhistle, to prevent cattle rustling. This set of circumstances conjures up the intriguing possibility of periodic cattle rustling raids occurring across the river between the two tribes! However the raiding could not have been that frequent as conflict between the two tribes would have hindered trade and the development of Windwhistle, which is known to have continued as an agricultural settlement into the Roman period.

Roman Period 43 AD to 410 AD

The Romans were very active in the area. Several Roman coins have been found in the village (one of which was dated to 305 AD) and three Roman villas are known to have been built locally. There was a Roman villa at West Dean (now under the railway station) and another at East Grimstead and another at Clarendon although none have been found within the parish of Alderbury. It would therefore be likely that the settlement at Windwhistle would have come under the control or influence of the villa at East Grimstead, being the closest of the three known villas. This villa was excavated between 1914-24 and it was found to be a substantial aisled type building, unusually containing three bath houses. The size of the villa possibly reflected the prosperity of the area.

During the Roman period the settlement at Windwhistle maintained its agricultural character. The smallholding or farm as it now would have become would have served the local villa community. The majority of the finds from the Windwhistle site relate to the Roman period. The pottery evidence of the period from Windwhistle such as Samian Ware (2nd century), Oxford Ware and New Forest Ware (3rd/4th century) indicates continuity of settlement, international trade and increasing wealth during this period.

Samian Ware is a bright glossy red coloured type of pottery. It was only manufactured in Gaul, on a vast scale, from where it was then shipped throughout the Roman Empire. The pottery has been found on almost every Roman site. The presence of Samian Ware at Windwhistle would therefore suggest evidence of trade links with Gaul.

New Forest Ware was a range of fine table ware, dark or red in colour. As its name might suggest it was manufactured in the New Forest. Kiln sites have been found near Fordingbridge from where the pottery was distributed throughout southern Britain.

Oxford Ware was produced in the potteries around Oxford, it was typically a white colour. The potteries produced fine bowls and jars which were distributed across southern and central Britain on the new road network.

The finds suggest that by the Roman period the local trade network had become sufficiently developed to allow the inhabitants at Windwhistle access to high quality goods produced both nationally and internationally via the local market network. In this case it was probably centred on Old Sarum (called Sorviodunum during the Roman period) as the city of Salisbury had not yet been built. It is likely that the community would have traded agricultural surplus at the market such as grain, wool, hides, cattle and textiles for finer pottery from Gaul, the New Forest and Oxford.

During the Roman period the road network was improved and so there was less reliance on the river network. During this period the port at Hengistbury Head declined, in part, as it became easier to transport goods overland. It is known that there were at least four main roads radiating from Old Sarum linking with modern day Andover, Winchester, Dorchester and Shepton Mallet. One has not yet been found radiating south from Old Sarum linking with the Roman port at Bitterne (called Clausentum, as Southampton did not exist at this time) although there is some written evidence to suggest that one did exist. The suggested route was again along the ridge up to Witherington Down following the current A36. It would most probably have run past the settlement at Windwhistle. The road would have been important giving the community at Windwhistle direct access to the local trading network at Old Sarum and the port at Bitterne.

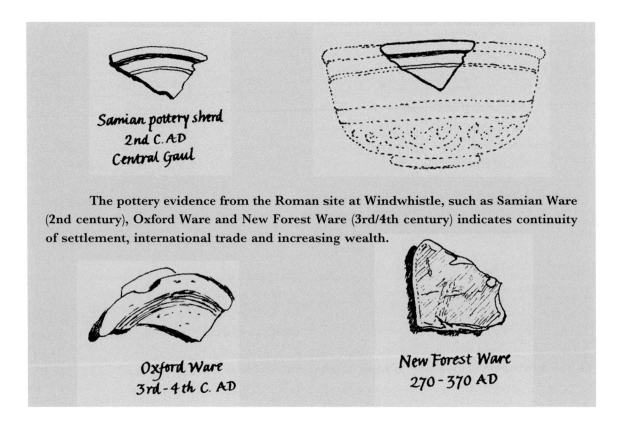

The pottery evidence from the Roman site at Windwhistle, such as Samian Ware (2nd century), Oxford Ware and New Forest Ware (3rd/4th century) indicates continuity of settlement, international trade and increasing wealth.

Early Saxon Period 410 AD to 800 AD

The Romans withdrew their legions in 410AD. It is not clear from the archaeological evidence as to what happened to the settlement at Windwhistle from the end of the Roman period. No finds have been found at Windwhistle dating to the Saxon period. Although this does not necessarily mean that the settlement was immediately abandoned at the end of the Roman period, as it is known that Saxon pottery does not survive well in the environment due to the generally poor quality of its fabrication. However there was plenty of medieval pottery found, a by product of manuring, suggesting that by this period the site was under the plough.

At some point during the Saxon period the site was abandoned, along with the other four ancient settlements, in favour of settlement at Whaddon and Alderbury. Or perhaps there was originally ancient settlement at both of these sites as well as the other five already mentioned but Alderbury and Whaddon came to dominate at the expense of the others. The growth of the villages may have eradicated any evidence of prior ancient settlement in the process. A church has been documented as being present initially in Alderbury and later in Whaddon (although there is no documented mention of a church in Whaddon until 1110 AD) which possibly made these two sites more important. The location of the churches could indicate that the other sites had been abandoned by this stage as churches would have been built within close proximity to the local population. Whatever the reality, both Alderbury and Whaddon are mentioned in the Domesday Book but a settlement site at Windwhistle is not mentioned and there had to be a relocation during this period.

It was known from the archaeological record that there was a strong Saxon presence in the area dating from the Early Saxon period. There is a large Saxon cemetery containing 71 burials at Petersfinger, which dates from the 5th Century. Perhaps some of the Saxon casualties from the early fighting with the Romano-British were buried in this cemetery. The Anglo Saxon Chronicles state that in 519 Cerdic (who was a Saxon leader who had led his army north from Southampton) fought the Romano-British near Downton. The Saxon advance then paused, for a generation at this point. It is not clear why this was the case but it took until 552 and a new generation led by Cynric, the son of Cerdic, to lead an assault on Old Sarum which resulted in its capture from the Romano-British. The parish of Alderbury would therefore have been on the border between the Romano-British and the new Saxon invaders for at least a generation.

In 1874 a Saxon burial was discovered in the banks of Witherington Ring by a game keeper digging out his ferret! The burial contained a long double edged sword, a spear and shield, possibly indicating the grave of a high status warrior. These items are now on display in Salisbury Museum. Unfortunately the burial is undated but its location may date it to the period of transition and the Saxon advance along the River Avon. It is not clear why seemingly this individual was buried alone rather than in a cemetery. However, it is common for individual Anglo-Saxon burials to be found on or near parish boundaries. The current parish boundary between Alderbury and Downton runs adjacent to Witherington Ring. The location of the burial would suggest that the bank marked a boundary in at least the Anglo-Saxon period if not earlier. It is possible, but there is no evidence, that it could have marked the boundary of the Saxon advance in the early 6th Century.

During the Early Saxon period the River Avon continued to mark a tribal boundary between two tribes. The area to the east of the river was known to have been occupied by the Jutes with the West Saxons occupying the region to the west of the river. By the later Saxon period the Jutes had been incorporated into the territory of the West Saxons and the region of Wessex.

Late Saxon Period (The Vikings) 800 AD to 1066 AD

The late Saxon period was characterised by the Viking invasion. No Viking raids have been documented as occurring in Alderbury. However, it is known that one such raid occurred nearby in Wilton in 1003 AD. The Viking army under Sweyn of Denmark plundered and burnt Wilton and then raided Old Sarum before returning to the coast and his longboats at Weymouth. It is speculation to suggest that the Viking invaders may have headed back to the coast along the River Avon from Old Sarum, past Alderbury, possibly raiding it en route!

Although Alderbury and Whaddon may have been subjected to the occasional Viking raid, it was likely that life changed very little in the area during this period, remaining

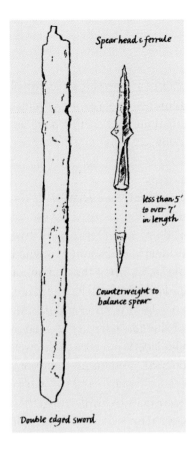

A long double edged sword, a spear and shield discovered in the banks of Witherington Ring was perhaps the grave of a high status Saxon warrior.

predominantly agricultural in nature. The region formed part of Wessex which managed to resist the Vikings until 1016 AD when King Canute, son of Sweyn, became king of England and Wessex was absorbed into his territories.

Within Alderbury there is physical evidence of Saxon occupation. It is more likely than not that there was a minster church built in Alderbury during the Saxon period where the current church now stands and the graveyard most likely contains Saxon remains. The WI History of Alderbury records that: *'Many Saxon remains were found when the road up from Longford Lodge to the church school was straightened out instead of curving round by Alderbury House. This must have been in the last half of the nineteenth century as it is recorded that the remains were all reburied in the present churchyard under Canon Hutchings' supervision'.* There is also evidence of Saxon earthworks to the north of the village which is also supported by the place name. The word 'bury' in Alderbury means an earthwork or fort.

The evidence would suggest that at some point during the Saxon period the village of Alderbury had become established as the primary settlement in the area. Its importance reflected in the fact that Alderbury gave its name to the Hundred in which it is situated thus making it the centre for the social, judicial and religious activities of the area.

Domesday 1086

The first written mention of Alderbury dates to 972 AD when the settlement is referred to as 'Aepelware Byrig'. The settlement is mentioned again in the Domesday Book (1086 AD) although the place name had changed to Alwar(es)berie. The entry makes reference to a church being located within the village. Whaddon is also mentioned in the Domesday Book as a village that could provide two men at arms, but as a tything of the parish, it was of less importance than Alderbury.

From the nomadic hunter gatherers of the Mesolithic period to the genesis of settlement some five thousand years later Alderbury and Whaddon grew to become well established communities.

The Rise and Fall of Ivychurch Priory

Situated on high ground to the north of the parish of Alderbury, within easy reach of the Royal Palace at Clarendon, Ivychurch Priory commanded a panoramic outlook across the surrounding countryside. In the 13th century it would have afforded its residents a stone by stone view of the building of the new magnificent Salisbury Cathedral in the valley below.

ABOVE *The pillar of Ivychurch Priory today.*

Ivychurch Manor

The Domesday Survey of 1086 recorded details of two distinct and separately owned manors within the Parish of Alderbury: Alderbury Manor and Whaddon Manor. An additional manor, the Manor of Alderbury Rectory, was created sometime between 1100 and 1122 when Alderbury Church, together with more than 100 acres of land and its dependent chapels of Ivychurch, Farley and Whaddon (all built after Domesday), were granted to the Bishop of Salisbury. Soon after 1139, the Priory of Ivychurch was founded, creating a fourth manor in the parish, probably with land from Rectory Manor. Although no foundation charter has been found, the earliest evidence comes from the Hundred Rolls of 1274, which names King Stephen as the founder. Later, in 1190 Alderbury Parish passed from

31

the jurisdiction of the Bishop to that of the Treasurer of the Cathedral and so became classified as a 'Peculiar'.

The Augustinians

Monasterium Ederosum, or Ederose, as the priory was then known probably because of the growth of ivy on the building, accommodated a prior and 13 canons. The small chapel already standing on the site, a dependent of Alderbury

> Sir Richard Colt-Hoare, the 19th century Wiltshire historian, records a story first published in a book in 1552, that workmen digging the foundations at Ivychurch discovered a mysterious tomb containing a book that they threw away as worthless. A curious individual retrieved the book but the only legible word was 'Prytannia' - hence, Britannia - for Britain. It has not been possible to prove the accuracy of this story.

Church, was incorporated into the new buildings and became the priory church. The priory followed the rule of the fourth century St Augustine of Hippo. The Augustinians, or 'Austins' as they were called, came to England after the Norman Conquest and set up a large number of their houses on a variety of sites across England and Wales. Their black-robed canons were priests who spent much of their time in the community looking after the spiritual well-being of ordinary people. However, when the Royal Family and its entourage were in residence at the nearby

Clarendon Palace, the canons of Ivychurch served in the royal chapels. The priests would have walked along the Canonsweye, a path that led directly from the priory to the palace, through the palace grounds.

The Layout of the Priory

Today, just a few ruins indicate the layout of the priory. In 1888, when a converted priory building that had been, at various times, a mansion house, a school and a farm, was demolished due to its dilapidated state after a fire, some interesting evidence came to light. There were found:

'Considerable remains on the south and the refectory on the north. The monks' cells probably originally connected the two, forming three sides of a quadrangle. The refectory was a noble room 40ft. by 18ft. The original moulded timbers of the roof were found, and the whole of the east end was covered with a large fresco of the twelve Apostles. Of the church, two Norman columns and

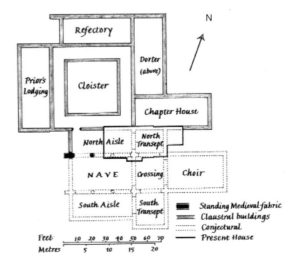

ABOVE *Plan of the Priory*

ABOVE *Ivychurch Priory today.*

part of the arches are still to be seen, and a doorway of later date. The bosses of the roof were to be seen in the ceiling of the bedrooms built over the church. With the exception of the columns and doorway of the church, the whole of this interesting building has been levelled to the ground'.

It is probable that the north aisle of the church adjoined an open cloister through a doorway. Around its perimeter, in addition to the refectory where the monks dined, there was a chapter house, a small chapel and the prior's accommodation. A kitchen and bakery adjoined the refectory at ground level together with a warming room. The dormitories would have been on the floor above.

Thomas à Becket's Visit

In January 1164, Henry II convened a Great Council at Clarendon Palace to discuss the 16 proposals of his new Constitution aimed at reducing ecclesiastical interference in the secular laws of England. The king had enabled Thomas à Becket, once his close friend, to become the Archbishop of Canterbury. Once in post, however, Thomas saw himself primarily as the servant of God and the church. He gave up a luxurious lifestyle for a humble and devout one. Thomas continually thwarted the king's plans and at the time of the Clarendon Council, he and the king were in a state of great hostility towards one another. Legend maintains that he wisely decided to lodge with the Prior and canons at Ivychurch Priory. Despite the many good things in the new Constitution, Thomas could not bring himself to ratify a proposal that limited the power of the church. This angered the king and Thomas had to flee back to a place of refuge in France. Eventually, with the king's permission, he returned to his duties at Canterbury Cathedral, only to irritate the king even more. Henry's petulant cry of *'Who will rid me of this turbulent priest?'* led to Thomas's violent death at the hands of four knights, within the walls of the cathedral itself - a murder not intended by the king who remained penitent for the crime for the rest of his days.

Priory Privileges

The priory enjoyed land privileges in Clarendon Forest granted by a succession of royal patrons, although they were never of very great value. From 1155, until the reign of Henry VIII, every king allowed alms of one and a halfpence a day, paid by the Sheriff of Wiltshire, rising by an additional penny a day from 1178 to an annual 100 shillings before dropping again.

When a new royal chapel was built in Clarendon Palace in 1236, King Henry III granted 50 shillings for another chaplain, and when repairs to the priory were needed, oaks from the forest were made available. In 1237 he ordered the bailiff of Clarendon: *'Not to vex, or permit others to vex, the priory in its enjoyment of herbage and pasture in the forest'*.

In 1248 he granted the right to 'agist' (to care and feed without charge) 20 pigs and their young, provided they were ringed in their noses so that they could not dig. In 1252 he gave the priory 60 acres of pasture rights at Sandcroft for their plough beasts. There were several more grants of land in the 14th century, the most important being that of the Manor of Whaddon with the advowson of its church, where the canons were obliged to say mass three times a week until its final abandonment.

A Shortage of Cash

Although by 1473 the Priory held at least 740 acres of pasture and wood on the forest and park, none of this could be converted into ready cash. Revenues, mostly small in value, came from Laverstock, Shrewton, Salisbury, Barford St Martin, Downton, Grimstead, Winterslow, Alderbury and Tilshead and the priory also owned a fulling mill at Mumworth (near Dairy Bridge) in Laverstock. There were also spiritual revenues from churches, wholly or partly appropriated to Ivychurch, and bequests and legacies in return for prayers, but the priory remained relatively poor.

A Light in the Night

King Edward II gifted 100 shillings per annum, to be paid by Clarendon Manor, *for finding a light burning forever in the monastery'* which the keepers of the manor found impossible to fund. After some years of friction, the prior complained to the King and Council. The dispute was eventually settled by an order for the money to be paid from the rents of Chippenham and Rowden.

The Black Death first arrived in England at Melcombe Regis, Weymouth, on the Dorset Coast, in the summer of 1348. Modern research has shown that the disease was brought ashore by a particular species of black rat travelling aboard merchant ships. These rats were host to a plague bacilli-carrying flea. The disease spread rapidly, passing through village, town and city, bringing death in its wake. The plague reached London in the autumn of 1348, flourishing in the unsanitary conditions of the densely packed population. By winter it had developed a pneumonic form affecting the lungs and spread by airborne droplets. Death usually occurred within a few days of the first symptoms appearing. It has been estimated that some 30-45% of the population of England, Wales and Scotland was wiped out. The community at Ivychurch Priory was gravely affected.

The Black Death 1348-49

The bubonic plague that swept across Europe in the summer of 1348 devastated the company at Ivychurch Priory. The Prior and 12 canons succumbed (and probably others in the local community too, but there is no written evidence of this). Only one of the canons, James de Groundewell, survived. He informed King Edward III of the situation and as no election of a new prior could take place in the circumstances, the king appointed James de Groundewell to the office. Even so, official visitors from the General Chapter of Austin Canons reported that no religious life of note was taking place. In 1349 new canons were sent, but the decline in standards continued.

A Disgraceful Episode

The prior who survived the plague, James de Groundewell, resigned in 1350, and his elected successor, John de Langeford, who resigned in 1357, amazingly took part in a most disgraceful robbery. In 1356, together with a company of canons and assisted by two lay persons, they broke into the property of Joan, the widow of the knight, John de Grymsted, at West Grimstead. They assaulted her servants at Alderbury, carried off her goods and also her bondmen. A royal mandate giving powers of arrest went out to all sheriffs, mayors, bailiffs and other ministers, as they became hunted vagabonds wearing secular clothes. This is an example of the unscrupulousness of canons during this time.

More Economic Difficulties

By 1399 the priory community numbered only two canons. A few years later it had fallen into such financial difficulties that there was little enough money to sustain even the basic necessities of life, having lost many of its endowments. Prior Rowde, in 1412, appealed for royal protection. This was granted by the Crown in respect of money for maintenance and discharge of debts. However, the poverty of its finances continued. In 1423 Henry VI granted to the priory the possessions of the church of Upavon and its dependent chapel at Charlton, on certain conditions. Over the following years measures were implemented to

> ## The gross valuation of Ivychurch Priory 1536
>
> *Credits*
> **£132.17s.10d   plus £14.10s 0d**
>
> *Ornaments, plate, stocks & stores*
> **£183.11s.0d,**
>
> *Woods*
> **£136.4s.2d.**
>
> **Most of the church building was eventually demolished.**

aid recovery and gradually the financial situation of the priory improved.

The end for the Priory

In 1534, the Act of Supremacy made Henry VIII Supreme Head of the Church of England. It allowed him to disband monasteries, priories, friaries and convents. Their ecclesiastical assets and income were redirected to the Crown. In 1536 Ivychurch Priory, as one of the 243 smaller houses having an annual income of less than £200 per annum, was one of the earliest foundations to be dissolved. The Returns of the Commissioners reported that the church, mansion and outhouses were: *'In a very good state with much new building of stone and brick.'* The household at that time comprised the Prior, five canons, one novice, five children *'for the church'*, a schoolmaster, four household officers and four waiting servants.

Prior Richard Page had to accept its fate: to have done otherwise was to risk imprisonment or even execution. In lieu of a pension he accepted the Rectory and Prebend of Upavon.

New Landlords

Within a year the manor was leased to Robert Seymour (uncle to Jane Seymour, who was Henry VIII's third wife and mother of Edward VI). In 1551 it was transferred to the Bishop of Salisbury and his successors (except during the Commonwealth) and leased to the Earl of Pembroke. The buildings were converted into a mansion house by Henry, 2nd Earl of Pembroke. The poet, Sir Philip Sidney, brother-in-law to the Earl, is said to have spent some time at Ivychurch and is believed to have written much of his famous poem 'Arcadia' there.

With the restoration of the monarchy in 1660, the manor was returned to the Bishop of Salisbury and leased to various families. The last lease was to the 1st Viscount Folkestone in 1757 and purchased outright by his grandson, the 2nd Earl, in 1801. From 1830 until 1862, the house was leased as a school 'Ivychurch Academy', run by the Sopp family.

Up in Flames

In 1888, the mansion that included much from the old priory was demolished following a fire. A farmhouse was built on the site of the north transept and north aisle. Built into its west wall are a number of sculpted fragments. Part of the priory and church complex remain standing within a few yards of the west wall of the farmhouse.

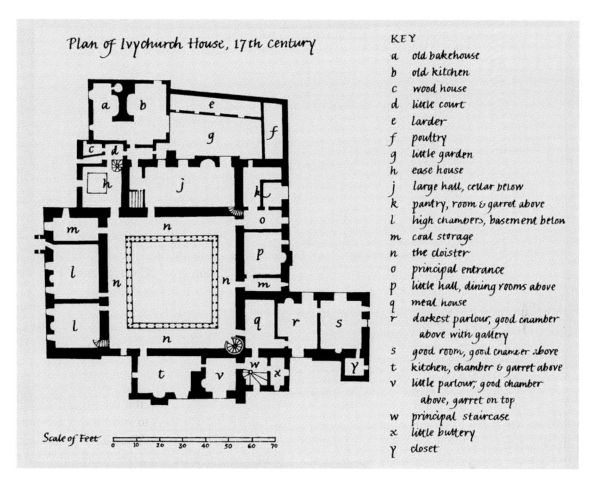

Plan of Ivychurch House, 17th century

KEY

a   old bakehouse
b   old kitchen
c   wood house
d   little court
e   larder
f   poultry
g   little garden
h   ease house
j   large hall, cellar below
k   pantry, room & garret above
l   high chambers, basement below
m   coal storage
n   the cloister
o   principal entrance
p   little hall, dining rooms above
q   meal house
r   darkest parlour, good chamber
    above with gallery
s   good room, good chamber above
t   kitchen, chamber & garret above
v   little parlour, good chamber
    above, garret on top
w   principal staircase
x   little buttery
y   closet

Scale of Feet   0 10 20 30 40 50 60 70

The site is not open to the public and currently is a working farm on private land.

TOP *Plan of Ivychurch House*
ABOVE *Ivychurch House shortly before demolition.*

37

Running the Parish

The Parish Council

The Local Government Act of 1894 established parish councils, the lowest rung of local government and the closest to the residents of the parish. This Act marked the end of church control of parish affairs. On 31 December 1894 the ten elected, voluntary members of the first Alderbury Parish Council met together. The posts of chairman, vice chairman and clerk were chosen. The new council's first task was to obtain the parish map that was in the possession of 'Squire Fort', to ascertain the exact boundaries and the rights of way. One major concern at the time was the inadequate water supply from various springs and dip wells. From 1906 the parish council became concerned with the dangers presented by the speed of the new motor vehicles (some things never change!). Despite repeated appeals to the county council, it was not until the 1930s that the roadside banks were cut back, pavements constructed for pedestrians, and corners widened and rounded near blindspots. In 1929 the council exchanged the old gravel pit on the Pitton Road, near Pope's Bottom, for the long term lease of the land that is now the Recreation Ground, from the Longford Estate. Today we can appreciate the wisdom of this move. In 1965, the council fulfilled a long held promise – to attach nameplates to roads.

The Local Government Act of 1972 gave parish councils wider powers and responsibilities in overseeing and serving the interests of their residents, although closely regulated. The councils are funded through a compulsory 'precept' that forms part of the Council Tax. For over a century, in times of peace and war, of national celebration and also of mourning, generations of parish councillors have given generously of their time to the benefit of the parish. Recently, after extensive consultations with villagers, the Alderbury Parish Council has drawn up a 20-year Parish Plan. Only time will tell if its proposals, reflecting the concerns, hopes and needs of the local community, will come to fruition.

Until recent years where the boundary lay affected where some villagers had to go to record their votes, but now, with only one polling station in use for the whole parish, the demarcation line is insignificant. However, among residents there still remains a strong, but good humoured, debate.

Policing the Community

In the early nineteenth century, social unrest, theft and sheep stealing were so bad in the Alderbury area, that Lord Radnor and other landowners formed a small private police force to patrol the locality.

In 1839, Wiltshire became the first county in the country to be authorised by Parliament to form its own constabulary. Alderbury's first paid constable was appointed in 1840, one of approximately 200 throughout the county. They had to be able to read and write, undertake long foot patrols late at night,

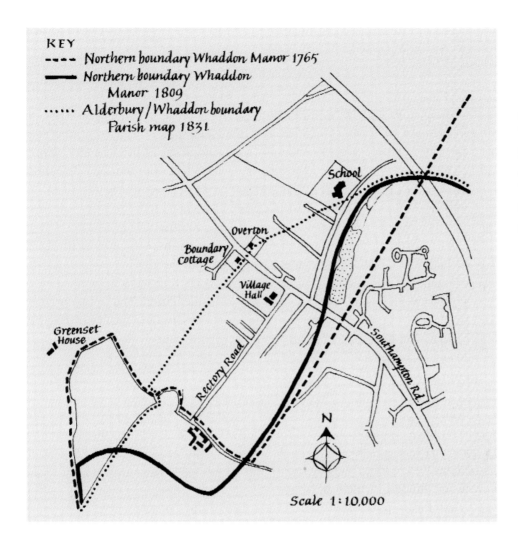

KEY
- - - - Northern boundary Whaddon Manor 1765
━━━━ Northern boundary Whaddon Manor 1809
...... Alderbury / Whaddon boundary Parish map 1831

School

Overton

Boundary Cottage

Village Hall

Greenset House

Rectory Road

Southampton Rd

N

Scale 1:10,000

LEFT

The boundaries between Alderbury and Whaddon throughout different eras.

and be always on call in all weathers. Bicycles were not available until the end of the century and the familiar helmet was not adopted until 1879.

The first police station was at Ivychurch Cottage on Old Road. In 1930, a county station, with family living accommodation, was built next to St Mary's Hall. As the area covered by the police station increased, another police house was rented in Firs Road in 1938. The old county police station was sold in the 1980s, and replaced by a new one on Grimstead Road. Officers based here now cover Alderbury and Whaddon and the surrounding areas.

Telephones

Although Lord Radnor had one of the first telephones some time between 1897 and 1904, they did not come into use in the village until 1923. A call office was opened by the Post

Office in Old Road – this would have been a telephone or kiosk connected to the manual switchboard in Salisbury.

As usage expanded, in 1928 an exchange was installed in the post office itself, with a switchboard and operator. There were 21 exchange lines and 24 telephone sets connected.

By 1946-7 it had been replaced by an automatic exchange with 81 lines and 102 telephones connected. New sets had dials so that the subscriber could dial other local numbers without using the operator. The exchange was located in the old timber yard, off Southampton Road on the site now known as Silver Wood. It relocated to Junction Road in 1978 and a new electronic exchange came into use. Alderbury numbers, once three digits, became six with the prefix 710 added (some now have the prefix 711) and in 1989 a digital exchange replaced the electronic one.

Alderbury Telephone Subscribers in 1928

Alderbury	1	Maidment Mrs., Sub-Postmistress	Alderbury P.O.
Alderbury	2	Folkestone Rt. Hon. Viscount	Alward House
Alderbury	21	" " " "	Estate Manager
Alderbury	3	Everett Maj-General. Sir H.J.	Avon Turn
Alderbury	4	Radcliffe Mrs. C.	Balderstone
Alderbury	5	Mould Ernest	(private) Alderbury
Alderbury	6	Ord W.W.	St Mary's Grange
Alderbury	7	Ruston Maj.W	Alderbury Holt
Alderbury	8	Wilts Co. Constabulary	Alderbury
Alderbury	9	Williams A. Sand Merchant	Heatherfield
Alderbury	10	Adams H.D.	Hillside
Alderbury	11	Three Crowns Inn, Commercial Garage	Whaddon
Alderbury	12	Davies Mrs A.L.	Belmont
Alderbury	14	Starling Rev. A.C.	Vicarage
Alderbury	15	Greenwood T.	High Trees
Alderbury	16	Fort E.M.	Alderbury House
Alderbury	17	Christie-Miller S.R.	Clarendon Park
Alderbury	18	Parsons E.A. Motor Engineer	Bridge Garage, Whaddon
Alderbury	19	Ald & Dist, Nursing Association	Ivy Cottage, School Hill
Alderbury	20	Hand F. & Sons, Sand Merchants	Whaddon
Alderbury	22	Mitchell A.E. Farmer	Witherington Farm

FAR LEFT *On the corner of Folly Lane by the bus stop.*

LEFT *Modern telephone box until recently near St Mary's Hall.*

Lighting Up

Even in this age of television, computers and fast worldwide communication, there are people living in the village today who can remember the time when there was no running water, electricity or gas, to provide heat and light and no sewage system. It is only when severe weather conditions cut our power supply, or freeze the pipes, that we can empathise with earlier generations.

Gas and electric power came to Alderbury and Whaddon in 1933-4. In 1933 the Wessex Electricity Company enabled homes to be wired up, but only for lighting, until the supply was linked to the National Grid a year later. About the same time, Salisbury Gas Company laid a gas main through the village. This provided manufactured gas until the country changed over to North Sea gas in the 1970s. It must have seemed like a miracle to have instant heat, light and cooking facilities at the flick of a switch or the twist of a knob. The parish council had five gas lamps erected along the main road at bus stops but these fell into disuse due to the lighting restrictions of World War II. (The old gas lamp at the corner of Light's Lane was sold for 50 shillings in 1963).

Flushing Down

Before 1964, when people went to the shed at the end of the garden, it was not always to find a spade! In 1950, the parish council complained to the Director of Education that Alderbury School still had bucket lavatories. He promised that they would be cleaned out twice a week instead of only once! Geoff Hatcher, an Alderbury resident, remembers that they were still using buckets when he left the school in 1964. In fact, the provision of public sewers was

41

not completed until 1964 and some houses still used bucket toilets after that date. There were several kilometres of sewers with four pumping stations connected to the Salisbury Sewage Treatment Works at Petersfinger.

The Turn of the Tap

The erection of The Fountain on The Green in 1902, in addition to commemorating the Coronation of King Edward VII, also marked

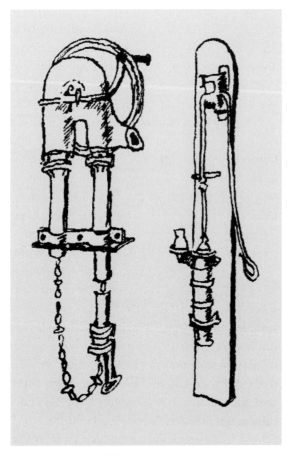

ABOVE LEFT *Chain lift pump*
ABOVE RIGHT *Lift and force pump*

Alderbury's appreciation of Lord Radnor making available a water supply to the village.

Prior to that water was obtained from wells, both public and private, and by rainwater collected from roofs into large iron tanks, some of which were buried with a pump on top. There appears to have been one of these at the rear of the Green Dragon, with part of a Lift and Force Pump attached to the rear wall. The two main public wells were in North Field behind Silver Street just above Alward House, and in Moor Field just below Totterdown Cottage in Folly Lane. This latter was served by a Chain Pump, which is an endless belt with discs attached. In addition there were a number of 'dip wells', these were springs into which a jug or similar receptacle could be dipped; the supply to these tended to be seasonal. One of these was on the north side of Folly Lane between Totterdown Cottage and Yew Tree Cottage; it re-appears as a spring in wet weather. Another was off Clarendon Road, down the track between Oak Lodge and Hillside House.

From the inception of the Parish Council in 1894, water supplies were continually a matter for discussion. In 1895 they obtained an estimate:

'*Sinking a well in the pasture by the garden wall of Ivychurch House, erecting a pump in the allotment field at the highest point for 30,000 gallons, laying mains, and erecting 8 patent self-closing, anti-freezing pillar fountains, for approximately £800*'.

This proved to be unaffordable. Interestingly a neighbouring copse behind the present-day forge has been shown on maps since at least 1849 as Pump House Plantation, so presumably at some earlier time there had

ABOVE *The pump still found on the corner of the High Street.*

been a pump there, probably for Ivychurch House.

In the event, in 1902 Lord Radnor paid Messrs Merryweather & Sons to pump water from a seemingly inexhaustible well at Longford Castle up to a reservoir with a 50,000 gallon capacity in the field above Ivychurch Farm. This head of water supplied all the floors of the castle and enabled fire hoses to have the pressure to reach the top of the castle from the ground. At the same time he provided a water main through Alderbury to a number of standpipes around the village. One of these survives in the hedge at the corner of High Street and Folly Lane. A recess for another one

is in the wall below the house at the junction of Folly Lane and School Hill. There were others in Southampton Road beside the steps leading up to Old Road, in the bank at Ladysmith Cottage on the Green, in Silver Street just below what is now Silverman's Cottage, and another in Silver Street adjoining the left-hand side of Rookwood. Besides having a tap for the villagers' use, these standpipes also had hydrant connections for use in the event of a fire in the village; if this occurred Longford Castle's supply could be cut off to increase the pressure.

In addition to the taps around the village there was also The Fountain, constructed in part from medieval pillars from Ivychurch Priory, with its water trough for horses. It also had taps on each side with iron cups attached by chains for people to drink the water (these latter have long since gone).

For quite some time the problem was eased. However, early in the 1950s, the Longford Estate decided not to undertake to supply water to Whaddon when a new estate of houses was planned. Instead, in 1952, the Rural District Council arranged for West Hants Water Company to supply piped water from a reservoir at Standlynch. After a public enquiry in 1954, it was agreed that the whole problem would be solved if the Longford mains were taken over by the RDC and piped water supplied to the rest of Alderbury. But this did not happen until 1956 when, as a consequence of a protest about the lack of water supplies from the residents of Folly Lane, High Street and the old Chapel area, the RDC obtained ministerial sanction to go ahead with the work.

Information from the records of Wessex Water, the current suppliers, show that substantial mains were laid in 1960 to install

43

sufficient distribution pipe-work to the established properties along Southampton Road, to the south-west of Alderbury and through to Whaddon. In 1997 much of the spine water main was re-laid in modern plastic material with a larger diameter.

ABOVE LEFT *The opening of the water supply in Alderbury 1902.*

LEFT *The Fountain on The Green today.*

The Home Front in World War II

The Arrival of the Evacuees

On 11 September 1939 when the old Alderbury School reassembled for the autumn term following the outbreak of war, Mr Carr, the headteacher noted in his logbook that the school roll had increased from 74 pupils to 184. The evacuees had arrived! The whole of Lyndhurst Road Junior Boys, Portsmouth, some girls, plus the staff, had been allocated to his small village school.

At that time Alderbury School was an all-age, infant to senior school. The addition of a whole school of junior boys and other evacuees besides, caused problems of space and many children had to sit three to a desk. To ease the problem, the Wesleyan Methodist Sunday Schoolroom at the top of Folly Lane, was hired to accommodate the senior pupils.

ABOVE *Group of evacuee children including Ronald Brett*

A Country Childhood

Anne Irving was a 12-year-old evacuee from London. She arrived with her mother, sister and cousin. They lived at Hillside Cottage (now Long Close) on Clarendon Road. It was a former gardener's home, rented from the Shallcross family who lived in the large house at the end of the drive opposite. Anne remembers wartime in Alderbury as a very happy time for their family. The cottage was snug and although they had electricity in the living room, candles were used elsewhere. There was an apple tree in the narrow garden that abutted the bank and in the nearby woods, where in spring daffodils and bluebells abounded, there were partridges and pheasants, inspiring in her a life-long love of nature.

The Shallcross family housed two other evacuees, Pauline and Tilly, with whom the cousins became friendly as they walked home from school, often calling in at Viney's, the local shop on High Street. Anne recalls the bitterly cold winters when they went sledging on tin trays in deep snow. The local boys teased the evacuees until they learned to speak with the local Wiltshire accent. Quite often they saw American soldiers who goodnaturedly threw candy and gum to them from their trucks: sometimes the girls threw apples in return. Anne and her family went back to London in time for VE Day. They awaited her father's return from Burma after VJ Day when they lit huge bonfires in their garden to celebrate. Anne says that she has never regretted her wartime education and loved those years of a country childhood spent in Alderbury.

A Lonely Time

For some evacuees, separation from their loved ones was a very confusing and scary time. One such child was Ronald Brett who was aged nine when he was evacuated to Alderbury. In the company of another boy, he was billetted at a house in the High Street where he felt strange and unwelcome. Ronald recalls:

'Two days later on the Sunday morning, coming out of church, we learned that war, whatever that meant, had just been declared. Life soon settled into a routine with our return to school albeit a bit different to the one that we had been accustomed to, but there was all sorts of new things to see and get used to. At the back of the house were some great trees, great to climb but not so good to fall out of as I found to my cost getting a large scar for my trouble. I saw my first adder, I don't know who was the more startled, it or me.'

When his hosts needed his room for their own nieces, Ronald was moved to another house in Whaddon, near the sandpits:

'I was soon in trouble at school for mixing with the children of one of the local families who spent most of their spare time in a hewn-out cave in the sand. I had my first cigarette in there and my first caning at school for going in there after being told to stay away.'

Homesick and lonely, Ronald decided to run away to Southampton where his aunt lived. He didn't get very far from Whaddon:

'I asked a man on a bicycle if I was on the right road and after being taken by him to his house and given a meal by his wife, I realised that he was a policeman.'

Fortunately, this episode turned out well for Ronald. He was re-allocated to the home of a couple who made him feel very welcome and wanted. He stayed happily with them until the end of the war, even going with them, with the permission of his mother, when the couple had to move away to do war work in another town.

Adapting to Rural Life

Jean Lygo (neé) Serle was just a few weeks short of her ninth birthday when she was evacuated to Alderbury with her mother, her 12-year-old sister, Joyce, and a baby brother. They arrived by train with other families from South London and then came on to Alderbury by coach. Jean and Joyce were allocated to the home of an elderly couple with no children of their own who lived at Railway Cottages on Junction

ABOVE *Three teachers in Alderbury school garden, Mrs Scammel, Mr Lush and Mrs Machon.*

Road. Their mother and brother were placed separately in a house near the Green Dragon. Jean writes:

'There were three railway cottages. All the men worked on the railway. There was no gas, electricity or running water to the cottages, a wood-burning range in the kitchen provided the only heat and it was on all of the time. We always sat in the kitchen: we were never allowed into the living room. The one and only time I was allowed in there was when I had scarlet fever and waited for an ambulance to come and take me to Sarum Isolation Hospital. Oil lamps provided light downstairs and we had candles to light our way upstairs to bed at night. Water came from a well at the back of the cottages, which we used to fill a large barrel and from which, in turn, we drew water for cooking, cleaning and washing. I remember accidentally dropping the bucket down the well, stirring up the water and so making the well unusable for about a week..... I was extremely unpopular with all the residents of Railway Cottages!'

It was difficult for evacuee children to adapt to rural ways and many went back to their own homes during the early period of the 'phony war'. Jean's mother and brother were among them and then her sister, too, returned to London when she was old enough to start work. Jean stayed in Alderbury until 1943, returning home in time to witness the doodlebug attacks over London.

LEFT *V1, 'Doodlebug' or 'Buzz bomb'*

The School at Clarendon House

At the start of the World War II Mr and Mrs Christie-Miller offered Clarendon House in Clarendon Park as a residential school for evacuees. Some 45 to 50 children aged between five and fifteen and mainly from Portsmouth's George Street School, were accommodated there. The former servants' quarters became their dormitories. The Library, lit by a beautiful chandelier and lined with shelves and shelves of old books, became the classroom for the older children and the younger ones had their classes in a Recreation Room.

An unnamed contributor to the Wiltshire Federation of the WI book, 'Wiltshire Within Living Memory', describes his time at the Clarendon House school. His uncle was the headmaster and his mother looked after the girl boarders. During the autumn of 1940 the bombings became more frequent and at nights from their dormitories the children heard the rumble of guns and saw the glow in the sky of distant fires from coastal raids. Then, one morning just before dawn, in November 1940:

ABOVE *Group of evacuee girls at Clarendon*

48

'We lay in bed not daring to sleep. An aircraft flew low. Its engine was not British. A whine. A crash. An explosion. The building shook. Windows rattled. Bits of plaster fell about us. We tried to hide our terror…In the cold light of day we inspected the crater: six feet deep and 15 feet across – a circular hole in the ground with a neat bank of soil around it. It was only 300 yards from our dormitory!'

Julia Tanson (née Foster), aged 9, attended the school at Clarendon House from September 1941. Her father, a member of the Southampton Fire Service, had been killed by enemy action. She recalls:

'The older of Mrs Christie Miller's grandchildren had ponies and we used to see them out riding. I remember the horses were called Merrylegs, Barney and Daisy. Sometimes we used to see famous people arrive for a function. David Niven, Sarah and Diana Churchill, spring to mind. Soon after I arrived we had a radio. We used to listen to children's programmes…. We used to amuse ourselves in various ways. At Christmas we did two plays for our parents to see on their visit. Their transport was organised by one of the parents and they came by coach.'

There was plenty for the children to do at weekends in the lovely grounds of Clarendon Park including ball games, exploring the old ruins at Clarendon Palace where they found delicious wild strawberries, climbing a specially designated tree they called Tarzan, hide and seek, blackberry picking and 'spud' picking:

'We were taken to the potato field and whilst the horses ploughed up the potatoes, we gathered the potatoes, cleaning the little ones and eating them raw. The boys would put worms down the girls' backs and there was much squealing. But we enjoyed the change. I seem to remember the

two big plough horses were called Punch and Spitfire'

Similarly, Lavenia Bartlett (nee Godfrey) had happy memories of being evacuated to Clarendon House when she was 10 or 11 years old. Her father was in the Navy and her mother stayed at home in Portsmouth. She remembers that for emergencies their shelter was a trench dug on the front lawn:

' ….but I only remember using it once. It had sheep hurdles over the top. Boys loved it. Girls hated the creepy crawlies.'

She too remembers walking up the hill to Viney's, the shop on High Street, to buy sweets. The Green Dragon pub was her father's first port of call when he came to visit and:-

'Every Sunday as we walked to church, the local mums would bring their children to their front doors to wave to us.'

Lavenia was confirmed by the Bishop of Salisbury in Alderbury Church. She loved the beautiful park at Clarendon. On one of their long walks she says that she witnessed two aircraft having a 'dog fight' over their heads. One was shot down by Alderbury Gate and the pilot taken prisoner. One Sunday there was a fight between two aircraft while the children were on their way to church and they picked up bullets from the ground.

Refugees from the bombed cities

Philip Newman, who lived with his parents on Southampton Road on Salisbury's outskirts, helped to dig trenches for the shelters on the Greencroft. He remembers that at school, in the event of a bomb attack, the pupils glued strips of paper crisscrossed on to the windows to prevent glass being blown into the classrooms.

Philip's mother was in the WRVS and helped with evacuees when they arrived from Southampton and Portsmouth. There the bombing was so intense that people had to flee with whatever belongings they could carry. He writes:

'I remember seeing them on the Southampton Road with their household goods on various means of transport, hoping to find a safe area in Salisbury and beyond… Every occupied house had a blast proof wall made from breeze blocks attached to French doors or windows, which darkened the room… My father spent his night as a 'look-out' for enemy planes at the factory next to his garage. We had an air raid shelter, which my father bought to build in the garden, so strongly built that it was difficult to dismantle after the war! But very often we would just huddle under the stairs in the cupboard until the siren went - the all clear'.

Tony Cooper, who lived at Dairy Cottages in Clarendon where his father was a gamekeeper until being called up, had relatives from Southampton to stay with them throughout the war.

'When the bombing raids at Southampton were at their peak, we all used to stand in our garden to see the glow of the raging fires and the beams of the searchlights scan the night sky above Pepperbox Hill. Only in adult life do I understand the dread that must have gone through their minds. Following D-Day I recall accompanying them to their home. Their block of flats still stood whilst all around was razed to the ground.'

Refugees also came from London. Molly Hornby tells of the time when a young ATS girl came to the door to ask if they would take in her mother, a Mrs Clements, for a few days' respite from the London bombing. The families got on so well that the friendship endured for many years.

War on the doorstep

People got used to the restrictions of life during the war: personal identity cards to be carried at all times, food and petrol strictly rationed, coal shortages, lighting restrictions, sirens, bomb alerts, fires and, in the worst-case scenario, the real possibility of enemy invasion. It was necessary to be vigilant, reporting anything unusual to the police. Road markings were erased, signs and milestones were pulled up to confuse the enemy, and widespread blackout restrictions were enforced. The nation was inundated with leaflets and advertisements from the Ministry of Information advising on what to do during emergencies. Over 38 million gas masks were distributed. Anderson air-raid shelter kits made of corrugated steel for out-of-doors assembly were made available cheaply and free to those on low incomes. From 1942 families could obtain an indoor Morrison shelter that doubled as a strong table with steel top and legs, and flexible mesh sides. Molly Hornby writes:

'A siren warned us of air raids. There was little we could do in response - we had no air raid shelter at home or at the village school. I don't think we considered ourselves in much danger out in the country.'

In January 1941 a public meeting in St Mary's Hall decided that the parish should be divided into six regions with firewatchers appointed to cover each area. There was an excellent response to the scheme and 91 residents volunteered for the duty. Vera James, recalls that whilst living at Belmont Farm:

'Night after night waves of German planes flew over en route to blitz one or another big town. At the age of ten years I remember being afraid of that continuous drone and of spending many evenings on a mattress under the table in the living room which was considered to be a safe place. The Anderson shelter was used whenever the siren sounded. An ominous orange glow could be seen from Alderbury on the nights of the Southampton Blitz.'

The family moved to Hole Farm in 1942.

'Safety at Hole Farm meant down to the cellar from the kitchen, and blackout in the front and middle rooms was effected by drawing up the original built-in wooden shutters from the window sills.....We had milk, eggs, vegetables and fruit from the garden. Our Jersey cow, from among a mixed herd, provided milk from which mum made

ABOVE
Rationbooks and identity cards needed during the war.

butter; eggs were preserved in water glass preservative; delicious rabbit pies and stews and a chicken every now and then, supplemented the meat ration. Farmers were allowed to kill one pig a year for their own family's consumption. The local butcher from Whaddon, Mr Newell, came to slaughter the pig at Hole Farm. It was the usual custom for farmers to share a pig between them, twice a year....'

Digging for Victory

Vera was lucky to live on a farm. For most people food was very scarce. Britain struggled to become self-sufficient while the war at sea raged. Food rationing, a relic from the last months of the World War I, was quickly reinstated by the government. Ration books were printed for each person in the family who then registered with their chosen local retailers. People were encouraged to plant vegetables instead of flowers and a favourite slogan of the time was 'Dig for Victory'. Fortunately, many people in Alderbury had gardens or were members of the Allotment Association.

Saving for Victory

Money was urgently needed by the government to fund the production of weapons, ships, aeroplanes and tanks. The issuing of National Savings Certificates and War and Defence Bonds encouraged the nation to save for the war effort. Even schools set up saving schemes for their pupils. War Weapons Week, the Spitfire Fund, Save our Ships (SOS), Warship Week, Salute the Soldier Week and Wings For Victory, were events keenly supported.

In March 1942 the Salisbury Journal reported that the mayors of Salisbury and Andover had wagered £5 on which town could raise the most during Warship Week. This enthused the local community so much that at the closing ceremony on the final Saturday of the week, the Market Square in Salisbury was filled with over 6,000 people. Loud cheers went up from the crowd as the indicator - a figure of Nelson pointing his telescope to the appropriate amount - moved steadily upward. The £210,000 target was actually doubled to £420,039 in the final minutes, winning the Salisbury Mayor his wager. Alderbury's own contribution that week amounted to £2,877 gained from investments, a whist drive, a jumble sale, a social, a competition, a bring and buy event and the school savings' scheme.

Village Life in Wartime

Despite restrictions, village life continued as normally as possible. Local women's groups, sports teams and all the uniformed organisations carried on. The Women's Institute set up a fruit preservation centre for making jam and chutney. Village ladies sewed or knitted thousands of items for the Red Cross, Salisbury Hospital and the troops abroad. A Recreation Ground ban on the playing of games on Sundays was lifted for servicemen and women - the fact that the Recreation Ground was still in regular use saved it from being dug over by the authorities for growing food. The Bowls Club offered their facilities to soldiers. St Mary's Hall was an overnight sleepover venue for troops passing through (there was no Village Hall at this time) and the Reading Room, on Old Road, provided light refreshments.

'There were even more concerts, socials, dances, whist drives, children's parties etc., than before the war', Linda Tanner (nee Dove) enthuses: *'Alderbury and Whaddon were really*

TOP LEFT *George Pitcher, NAAFI manager 1942.*

TOP RIGHT *Mollie Robinson, Jimmy Clerk and Doreen Johnson.*

LEFT *Doreen Johnson, Barbara Robinson, Miriam Perry and Mollie Robinson.*

alive; dancing in the WI hut and in the NAAFI. The pubs ran out of beer lots of times.'

Molly Hornby writes: *'Girl Guide meetings carried on in spite of our Guiders, Lady Betty (Lady Elizabeth Pleydell Bouverie) and Miss Dorothy Stevens, joining the ATS at the start. When Lady Betty left the ATS she would come down from London to our meetings about once a month which were sometimes held at Greenset (on Vicarage Lane) where we made camouflage nets on the lawn and dyed our faded guide uniforms in one of the outhouses. Other meetings were held at Mrs Allen's house and garden in Clarendon Road where we 'dug for victory' - but not very successfully! When Miss Stevens returned from serving in the ATS she had a huge influence on the Ist Alderbury Company of Guides, invigorating them with new ideas and starting the Brownie Pack again.'*

Queen of the May

The tradition of Crowning the May Queen was an annual event throughout the war years. Linda Tanner particularly remembers May Day 1944 when she had the honour of being the May Queen. The fête was staged in aid of Salute the Soldier Week. The long procession included representatives of the Services, cadets, the Home Guard, wardens, Boy Scouts, Girl Guides, maypole dancers, and finally, the May Queen and her attendants riding in a gaily decorated pony and trap. Headed by a drum and fife band and buglers of the Army Cadets,

ABOVE *Linda Dove as May Queen in 1944 with her attendants.*

the procession made its way through the village. A host of events awaited them at the Recreation Ground: a baby show, a tug of war (won by an American team who refunded the prize money), displays by Army and Navy cadets, maypole dancing by the schoolchildren, a dog show, skittles, a darts competition, a rummage sale and teas. This wonderful, morale lifting day finished with a dance at the Hut organised by the Home Guard.

Alderbury & Whaddon Home Guard

Major General Sir Henry Everett, KCMG CB, of Avon Turn, Shootend, led the excellent Local Home Guard unit, Alderbury Company 7th Wilts, until 1942. The unit trained in any available safe space such as the field behind Old Road, the gravel pit, the timber yard, (now Silver Wood), Ashley Hill and land near Petersfinger. At this time the road that ran through the village was the main route to Southampton and Portsmouth. This, together with eight railway bridges and the railway line, needed protection. Defences included tank traps (so-called tiger teeth) which were made of concrete blocks with a hole in the centre. They were sunk across the road at intervals and laid to one side of bridges to stop enemy tanks crossing. Stakes were sometimes put into the holes to impede access. Large concrete blocks were laid at the side of the road and a deep ditch ran alongside the railway line.

A tragic event on Ashley Hill

On 13 September 1942, Lieutenant William Foster MC DCM, aged 61, of Hurstbourne House, Alderbury, a decorated and veteran soldier of the Great War and the South African War, was killed in an act of courage that saved the lives of many recruits. Their training involved the throwing of live grenades over a slit trench on Ashley Hill. Eleven grenades had already been thrown successfully, but the twelfth man slipped as he threw the grenade towards the top of the slope facing him. It rolled back towards Lieutenant Foster and several others. Giving an order to scatter, William Foster ran towards the rolling grenade and threw himself on it. It exploded and killed him instantly. For this courageous action he was awarded a posthumous George Cross and there is a special plaque in St Mary's Church in his honour.

Alderbury is bombed

Peggy Ling, (née) Eastman who grew up at Home Farm, recounts the frightening events of the times when Alderbury was bombed.

'In November 1940 a bomb fell on the Pitton side of Clarendon House in a field near the Wild Gardens. Then one summer night in 1941 a German bomber dropped its load over Alderbury as a British fighter plane chased it. The first bomb fell on the northeast lower side of Ivychurch Copse, but failed to explode. The site was found by village boys. The second one fell just below Ivychurch Farm, where the tennis courts are now. The plane flew on over Silver Street. A bomb was dropped each side of Home Farm. The one in the ditch blew the back doors open. A fifth one fell in a field near a clump of trees by a gravel road to Longford Park. The Lewis Gun on the top of the square tower of the castle failed to shoot the plane down. Southern Command stationed there replaced the gun with a larger Bofors gun camouflaged by a group

of bushes. Fortunately, there were no casualties. The military had to be accommodated in every available space. Large houses were taken over and private houses with rooms to spare..... The main camp was in the woods near Shute End. Tanks and lorries were parked in the side roads and under the trees. There was always tight security near the camps on the Lower Road and at the entrance to Longford Park. Different British units came and went. In 1944 the area was taken over by the American military. The USAMC General Hospital had been built at Odstock to take the expected invasion casualties, further increasing the American presence in Alderbury. The military police were everywhere.'

ABOVE *ATS girls, Mollie Robinson and Doreen Johnson, in a bomb crater.*

Serving with the ATS

Jane Knight was a captain in the ATS Royal Corps of Signals and stationed in Alderbury. She remembers that Longford Castle housed the local Hants & Dorset headquarters. The 'A' Mess anteroom was in the picture gallery there. 'B' Mess was in St Marie's Grange where she rang the bell in a bell tower after the victory at El Alamein - the first time bells had been rung in Britain since before the war. Alderbury House contained the Hants & Dorset Signals Mess where she was stationed, although due to the shortage of accommodation, she slept in a room at Mr and Mrs Freeman's bungalow on Oak Drive. The entire company of the ATS Signals unit was housed at High Trees on Light's Lane. The Southern Command ATS Officers Mess was in the North Canonry of Salisbury Cathedral where Jane 'messed' during her first months in the Command. According to Jane, life was not all hard work!

'There was a dance once a month that was strictly long dresses. All the officers were told to park their vehicles outside The Close, which was locked at midnight. Most disregarded the instruction so were locked in at midnight and were obliged to get the gatekeeper out of bed!'

Yanks in Alderbury

Molly Hornby's grandparents had five soldiers from the Tank Corps billeted with them at Shute End Farmhouse:

'The Americans came later and were fewer in number. I can remember being chatted up by a couple of young G.I.s at our garden gate at Belmont. I was 15 at the time and resisted their efforts to get me to go to the cinema with them... Also at Belmont Farm we had a group of Italian

prisoners of war digging out the 'big ditch' which ran right through the fields, parallel to the river and controlled the water levels in the meadows by means of a series of hatches. I was not allowed to go anywhere near them but my father reported that they seemed glad to be out of the fighting and that they had caught and cooked hedgehogs!'

Eileen Eyres (née Watson) lived at the Three Crowns, Whaddon, with her parents, Arthur and Kate Watson, and her Uncle Joe and Auntie Em Watson. When the Americans came they used a room in the inn as an Officers' Mess and they also took over the kitchen.

'We had many food items given to us that were leftovers. I remember one birthday the American cook made a chocolate pie for me. The filling was so big that when the cook had left for the day to go back to camp, my mother took half out and made a second pie. When I had measles two young assistant cooks helped to entertain me by reading stories and playing Snakes and Ladders... I also remember eating mashed banana and custard, only to be told years later that this was in fact cooked parsnips with banana essence!'

Linda Tanner and her friend Pam Horgan (née Barnes) remember the day when a German plane buzzed the school playground causing the children to run indoors and hide under their desks. Linda also remembers seeing General Eisenhower and Mr Churchill arrive at Longford Castle, the area headquarters of Southern Command.

On a wing and a prayer

From the evening of 5 June 1944 and all the following day, villagers watched wave after wave of aircraft, some towing gliders, flying towards

ABOVE *The address presented to Mrs Joan Forrester and to all ex-service men and women.*

Europe. It was D-DAY, the day that Allied troops landed on the Normandy beaches for their final assault on Hitler's Europe. It was the beginning of the end of the war.

Welcome Home

At the end of the war, a Fund was formed for the ex-service men and women of Alderbury, Whaddon and Clarendon. On 19 May 1947, a Welcome Home Party was held in the hut of the HQ Army Cadet Force (Alderbury). Each of the 133 returnees was presented with a framed, illuminated address together with a gift of two pounds.

The Man Who Never Was!

The recollection of a wartime mystery by John S. Eyres

At some time in the 1930s, our firm of A.E. Eyres & Sons began to receive visits from a salesman whom I will call Mr A. I became aware of this early in 1938 when we moved house from Chuzzlewit down to Wisteria Cottage. Mr A usually arrived rather late in the afternoon and after his business discussions with my father and my uncle, my father often invited him to have cup of tea with us.

Mr A, who was not British, was a man of medium height and build with thinning brown hair and he was neatly dressed generally in a blue suit. Probably the most distinctive feature was that he wore rimless octagonal glasses supported on gold wire frames. Mr A, who seemed to be in his forties, told us that he lived in Dorset on the shore of Poole Harbour. I found his accent rather intriguing in those days, when I was not even a teenager. Then, of course, the war started in 1939 and all private building halted, and so Mr A's visits came to an end.

In 1940, after the fall of France, my father joined the Local Defence Volunteers. That September there was grave concern across the country over the possibility of a German invasion. The Home Guard set up checkpoints on many roads in the South of England, including one near the Three Crowns in Whaddon. My father went to that road block quite regularly for about two months until the invasion scare subsided. He took the four-hour watch from 8pm until midnight and my mother and I stayed up waiting for him to return.

On this particular night, father told us about a most surprising event. Among the vehicles that they had stopped and examined, was a military staff car. The occupants of the car included military personnel as well as hospital people and - most unexpectedly - none other than Mr A himself. This was so mysterious, that a foreign material salesman from Poole Harbour would be riding in a military vehicle in the middle of the night. What on earth was happening?

Well, more than 30 years later, I believe I came across the answer. I was on leave, staying with a relative in the Midlands, and read a book about the Twenty Twenty, or XX Committee, in the war. *(Editors' note: The title of the book is 'The Double Cross System in the War of 1939-45' by J.C. Masterman, who was Chairman of the Committee)* It described the exploits of German agents whose loyalty had been 'turned' to escape execution. One of the exploits exactly fitted the scenario that my father witnessed at the roadblock near the Three Crowns. The agent, whose name was omitted, but whose nationality was the same as Mr A's, had been driven to meet a German parachutist who had made a hard landing in Britain and had broken a leg. The narrative was a perfect fit to father's account and is undoubtedly the true explanation.

However, I wrote to Sir John Masterman, the author. Sir John did reply, but he categorically denied that the incident in his book ever took place near the Three Crowns.

In conclusion, I may add that I saw another edition of the book, published nine or ten years later - and guess what?... The entire account of the parachutist with a broken leg was totally omitted!

Editors' note: Apparently, information about the Double Cross System remained secret after the war and British Intelligence initially refused authorization for the publication of the book in 1961 and again in 1970. Masterman then published in America. Eventually, permission was granted in 1972, provided there were some omissions from the original text. Could one of them be the exploits of Mr A?

ABOVE *Coronation celebrations in Old Road in 1937.*

The Group has produced a book regarding those who lost their lives in both World Wars entitled 'Alderbury War Memorials - In Freedom's Cause'.

Then and Now

ABOVE *Court House.*

RIGHT *Jasmine Cottage 1930's.*

ABOVE *Court House today.*

LEFT *Jasmine Cottage, a recent photo.*

ABOVE *The old school in 2011.*

RIGHT *Old post card of Alderbury school.*

LEFT *The High Street from Folly Lane 1998.*

BELOW *The High Street in 1912.*

High Street and Wesleyan Church Alderbury 113.

ABOVE *An old post card showing the High Street looking towards Folly lane.*

RIGHT *The same view today.*

ABOVE *Rose Cottage 2011.*

LEFT *Rose Cottage in 1920.*

ABOVE *The old
railway bridge
being removed.*

RIGHT *The same
view in 2011.*

ABOVE

*The Old Post
Office Cottage
in 1956.*

RIGHT

*The Old Post
Office Cottage
in 2011.*

Whaddon.

Manor Farm, Whaddon.

TOP *Matrons College Farm 1906.*

LEFT *Matrons College Farm today.*

OPPOSITE TOP
An old post card of Southampton Road, Whaddon.

OPPOSITE BELOW
A similar view in 2011.

RIGHT

Ladysmith Cottage, The Green, 2011.

BELOW

Ladysmith Cottage circa 1928.

ABOVE
*Silvermans
Cottage, Silver
Street in the late
1800s.*

RIGHT *The same
view in 2011.*

Readin, Ritin 'n Rithmetic - The Path to Literacy

Before 1800 and through early Victorian times there was little intent on the part of the government to set up a national system of education. Some even thought that the best security for the existing social order would be to discourage the working class from getting any education at all. According to one MP, they would *'despise their lot in life'*. Child labour was common and working class parents, too, were often reluctant to give up their children's earnings. So, the path to literacy was a painfully slow, halting process that took most of the 19th century to achieve.

Alderbury School

The Anglican *National School Society for the Education of the Poor in the Principles of the Established Church* (founded 1811) and its non-conformist rival, the *British and Foreign School Society* (founded 1814), encouraged wealthy local benefactors to provide voluntary schools for the poor labouring classes.

William, the third Earl of Radnor, founded an elementary school in Alderbury for the local poor children in 1838. Although the Radnor family came from Huguenot origins, William was an Anglican, and with the enthusiastic support of the local vicar, Rev. Newton Smart, it was almost inevitable that it would become a National School (as it did by 1848 or even earlier). The building selected for the school was once a farmhouse situated on what is now called School Hill. Originally it was a medieval hall house and it was extended to incorporate a large schoolroom. The 1838 date stone is on the north gable. The old part of the house accommodated the schoolmaster. An extension in the 1850s added a further classroom. An HMI report of 1858 said that it comprised:

'Three rooms (1)42x20x8½ (2)27x20 x8½ (3)12x 20x8. 115 scholars, mixed, under master (certificated) and sewing mistress who teaches the little ones in an upper room. Three pupil teachers, desks parallel, floor boarded. Mr Hughes said that the discipline and instruction were very good'.

Teacher training

In 1846, with a shortage of qualified teachers, a five-year pupil-teacher training scheme was brought in by the Government. Able children of thirteen or over could combine daily teaching sessions under the supervision of the headteacher, with out-of-hours tuition. Their work was officially inspected every year and, if satisfactory, both headteacher and pupil-teachers would receive grants worth £10, rising to £20 a year. After five years the students could apply for training college or stay at the school as unqualified assistants, while, perhaps, studying for a teacher's certificate. Several pupils from Alderbury School took up this opportunity. This afforded women especially, the chance of rising from poor labouring backgrounds into a secure profession with some status, a moderate income, and a pension.

HEADTEACHERS

Pre 1841 - Thomas Macintosh
Pre 1848 - 1851 John Frost *(died)*
1851 - 1866 George Burden
1866 - 1871 Thomas Bunston
1871 - 1900 Richard Knight
1900 - 1907 Edward Knight *(died)*
1907 - 1929 AT Freeman
1929 - 1952 JW Carr
1952 - 1974 George Murray
1974 - 1987 Anthony Smith
1987 - 1990 Enid Pope
1990 - 1992 Jack Copping

The Victorian classroom

Classrooms were generally gloomy with windows set high on the wall to avoid any distractions, and very cold in winter. Attendance was not compulsory, or free, until towards the end of the century and then only until the age of twelve. Children had to pay their school pence every week, an expense that large families could barely afford. In June 1887 the school log book records:

'Several children whose school pence has been paid by Mrs Hutchings, (the vicar's wife), having been irregular, it has been decided that all those children who bring their penny on Monday mornings, if they are regular during the week, will have their penny returned to them on Friday.'

Discipline was strict and it was usual for a cane to be displayed in a prominent place. Pupils brought their own lunch. One common cause of absenteeism was disease. Typhoid fever, measles, mumps, whooping cough, scarlet fever and diptheria were very infectious and Alderbury School had to be closed for this reason on several occasions, up to and including, the Second World War.

The Victorian Curriculum

The curriculum consisted mainly of a daily grind in the 3Rs, normally using the rote method of constant repetition. It was usual for infants to practise writing by tracing letters with their fingers or with sticks in a sand tray, progressing to scratching words and sentences on a slate with a slate pencil. At a later stage pupils mastered the art of copperplate handwriting using pens with scratchy steel nibs dipped into inkwells brought round by monitors. Reading was practised using charts with pupils repeating lists of words in unison. Arithmetic was taught with the help of an abacus. Sewing was compulsory for girls in the afternoons, and at Alderbury was usually taught by the headteacher's wife.

'Lady Folkestone and Miss Bouverie came to the school this afternoon. Her Ladyship heard the children sing and very carefully inspected the needlework, commending some and blaming others. Her Ladyship hoped to see great improvement on her next visit.' (school log book, November 1866).

The teaching of religion also permeated the day with bible pictures, maps and moral tracts displayed around the walls. The vicar would visit the school each week to teach the children their catechism and say prayers. A member of the diocesan clergy would come to test them once a year. In 1867 the infants' room above the main hall was demolished and a new classroom built on the ground floor. As a child's knowledge of the world outside his own local area was very limited, the curriculum was gradually expanded to include a range of other subjects sometimes taught in the form of 'object' lessons, e.g. coal, house, clay, bread, chalk, tiger, sheep, trees, elephant, iron, cotton etc.

Payment by results

From 1862 to 1890 grants were given to denominational schools on a 'payment by results' scheme. Every year each individual pupil over the age of seven was tested in the 3Rs by a visiting inspector. This not only brought great anxiety to the pupils but to the staff too, as the failure of the child to reach the required standard, together with an un-satisfactory attendance record, meant a possible reduction in the school's grant, and, consequently, the teachers' pay. Children were tested and retested as the dreaded Inspection Day loomed:

'Mr Hutchings (the vicar) *addressed the children on their duty to make a point of attendance on that day. Absence without good reason to be visited by raising the school fees of such absent child by one penny for the next half year.'* (school log book, November 1866).

ABOVE *A prefabricated mobile classroom accommodated the overflow pupils and was used later as the preschool.*

Into the 20th century

The Education Act of 1870 divided the country into school board districts, empowered to build new elementary schools where there was poor provision. Voluntary schools had to make good their accommodation within six months. In 1880 attendance was made compulsory for all children at least to the age of 10, and in 1893 the minimum leaving age was raised to 11. (It rose again to 12 in 1899 and to 14 in 1918.) In 1902 the Boards were superceded by county council authorities. In 1909 a new playground was opened and the schoolroom gallery was removed in 1911.

From National to Council School

It was over an issue of financing cloakroom improvements demanded by Wiltshire County Council in 1929, that Lord Radnor decided to make over the lease of the school to the local authority. So, for a nominal rent, Alderbury National School became a council school. Among the reforms of the 1944 Education Act provision was made for public education to be organised into three progressive stages: primary, secondary and further education, with separate schools for primary and secondary pupils. The leaving age was again raised to 15 (16 in 1972). It was not until July 1952 that Alderbury saw the end of its all-age school when it became the Alderbury County Primary School for the next 40 years. Pupils over the age of 11 could go on to Downton Secondary School, or by a selection test, to a Salisbury grammar school. In 1952 a school dinner service started with meals brought by van.

In 1972 a prefabricated mobile class-room was erected at the corner of Folly Lane and School Hill to accommodate rising numbers, and an outdoor swimming pool was erected on nearby ground by the Parent-Teacher Association. A computer made its appearance at the school in the late 1980s marking the beginning of a new technological age in education

The end of Alderbury School

In 1992, following the 1988 Education Act, a National Curriculum was brought in for all state primary and secondary schools, standardising the contents of the curriculum and enabling assessment and the compilation of school league tables. By this time, however, plans were well in hand for a new joint primary school with West Grimstead, made possible by the Salisbury Diocesan Board of Education together with an input of £35,000 from the two local communities. A site on Firs Road, Alderbury, overlooking the bypass, had been negotiated with the Earl of Radnor. At the end of the autumn term in December 1992, after a spate of reunions, school parties and a sad farewell service in St Mary's Church, the old school closed forever. In January 1993 the new Alderbury and West Grimstead, Church of England, Voluntary Aided Primary School opened its doors to welcome its first pupils.

The New Alderbury and West Grimstead CE.VA.School

The first head teacher, Stewart Blades, took on the onerous responsibility of planning, furnishing and stocking the new school. The new building was a source of joy to the pupils with its extra large, bright and airy hall fitted with an exciting range of PE equipment. Adjoining the hall was a modern kitchen providing meals prepared on the premises. The six classrooms were each named after a British bird or animal and they all had computers and cooking equipment. There was an impressive carpeted entrance hall, two library areas and a resource centre.

ABOVE *The entrance to Alderbury and West Grimstead School.*

Furthermore, the toilets were inside - no more dashing across the playground in the rain!

Sadly, Mr Blades fell ill and had to retire. The deputy headteacher, Mrs Tindle, took over until the new headteacher, Mrs Jennifer Pitcher, arrived in September 1995. Mrs Pitcher made her own distinctive mark, leading the school to a very successful Ofsted report in 1997. Friends of Alderbury and West

77

Grimstead School (FAWGS), the parent-teacher association, provided many extras including a portable stage, an outdoor play fort, and playground tables and seats. In 1998 it raised almost £5000 toward a Design and Technology extension. Soon an additional classroom was needed to accommodate rising pupil numbers and in November 2000, Bishop Peter of Ramsbury officially opened and blessed the new classroom - Year 5 'Dragonflies'. This meant that the school could now be organised with children in single year rather than mixed-age groups.

The years 2000 - 2010

A landmark was reached in 2003 with celebrations of the new school's 10th birthday. Staff, children and governors held a 'Big Picnic' in the hall which was decorated with giant birthday cards made by each class. Extensions to the office and staffroom during 2003 reflected the growing numbers of teaching assistants and the space needed for a Finance Officer as well as the Admin Officer. The village was delighted when a long-held ambition was realised in the summer of 2008 - the arrival and winching into place of the new mobile unit to bring Alderbury Pre-School onto the school site. After an enormous amount of organisation by the Pre-School committee, the new doors opened to under-fives in the September. It also took over the running of a Breakfast and After-School Club providing 'wrap around care', a much-needed facility for working parents. Having the Pre-School on the same site made it much easier to maintain close links and the younger children regularly visit the Early Years class, taking part in special school events such as the Nativity and Harvest services.

People

The whole community was greatly saddened by the death in 2002 of Graham Hunt, a wonderful and supportive governor who had been Chairman for many years. As a permanent reminder of Graham and also of young George Collins, who died tragically in a car accident in the same year, children's designs were integrated into a special memorial garden which was blessed by Bishop Peter in 2005. In the summer of 2010, three metal sculptures (a candle, a dove and a cross), crafted by Basil Elliott of Alderbury Forge to designs by one of the staff, were placed in the garden to create a quiet Sacred Space reflecting the school's values of friendship, thankfulness and service. The garden is a place of quiet and tranquility.

Mrs Jennifer Pitcher, who had been headteacher since 1995, left in the summer of 2005 to become a county adviser. The whole school community gathered to say goodbye with gifts and speeches at a large informal party on the field. The third Headteacher, Paddy Macey, previously the Deputy Head, took over in September 2005.

Keeping up to date

AWGS has always been a vibrant, creative place for children to learn, develop and thrive. Over the last ten years, five of the staff have been Leading Teachers for Wiltshire County and all staff are encouraged to further their professional development. The school has been very keen to embrace new technology and had soon installed internet access and invested in laptops (both for the staff and then later, a computer suite for the children), digital cameras, data projectors, video recorders (later superceded by DVDs) and Smartboards in each classroom. Thanks to the community, thousands of Tesco vouchers enabled the 'purchase' of many computers and other equipment. The school's first website was launched in September 2001 and rebuilt to a new design in 2007. Changes in education and a succession of government initiatives led to a curriculum that was always evolving - Ofsted and SIAS (Church Schools Inspection) reports in both 2002 and 2007 recognised AWGS as a 'good' school. In 2007 everyone was delighted to read what they already knew :

'Pupils' achievement is good and standards are above average by the end of Year 6. There is a strong sense of belonging, and pupils' enjoyment of school is outstanding.'

Learning outside the classroom

The children continue to benefit from a wide range of experiences - there are many visits to historic sites, the cathedral, the churches in Alderbury and West Grimstead, museums, the theatre, and other places. Visitors share their skills and knowledge such as sports coaches, artists, authors, poets, musicians and historical experts. There are themed days where great fun is had in dressing up. There are many different after-school and lunchtime clubs which have included football, cricket, netball, rugby, athletics, recorders, guitars, orchestra, gardening, painting, sewing, knitting, crafts, chess, board games, ICT and French, amongst others. Children take part in sports matches and tournaments, local junior area sports and mini-marathons and enjoy raising money for charity. The Y5 children spend three days each year on a residential visit at Braeside House in Devizes and the Y6 children spend three days away at

Oxenwood, near Marlborough; each group enjoying outdoor activities such as archery, wall-climbing, orienteering and a very long walk! A visit from the Story Box Theatre has become a regular fixture - a magical show using puppets to retell traditional tales. The visit of a pantomime group is a treat at Christmas. Another highlight is the annual Music, Art and Poetry Evening. The school hall is turned into an art gallery and any child who has instrument lessons at school is invited to play in public, with poetry written and read by the school's talented writers. Services at Harvest, Easter and Christmas are always a delight and are led by the children, as is the more reflective Re-membrance Service. Members of the clergy and church team are usually able to join the school at these special times as well as regularly leading worship once a week. Christmas sees the youngest children performing a nativity play as part of the service, while the older children work extremely hard with the staff to prepare and perform a musical based on the Christmas story - always a triumph!

Awards

The school is proud of several awards: AWGS was one of the first schools to achieve the Basic Skills Award recognising its work in Literacy, Numeracy and getting children started in their learning. The Arts Council twice awarded the school their Gold Arts Mark for excellent provision in the arts. There is the Healthy Schools Award for sports and, at the time of writing, staff and children are working towards a Green EcoMark reflecting a 'green' approach to living, and also the 'Sing Up' award.

Further afield

Children today are encouraged to consider life in other countries. French, German, Spanish and Swedish have been introduced and regular visits from Swiss, Danish and German students give the children an appreciation of different languages. For several years the school hosted Japanese students who brought a completely different culture. At the time of writing there are links with a school in China and a boy in a Brazilian school.

Parents and Governors

'Friends of Alderbury and West Grimstead School' (FAWGS) work tirelessly to promote social and fundraising events, providing the school with valued equipment, resources and funds. The Governors, likewise work extremely hard with the headteacher and staff, to ensure that the building is in good condition and that the school is well managed.

In 2010 the headteacher, Mr Macey, was appointed to the headship of a large Southampton school and his responsibilites were taken over, temporarily, by Ray Picton, as acting headteacher. Mrs Alison Small has been appointed as the new headteacher from September 2011.

LEFT *Part of the memorial garden at Alderbury and West Grimstead School.*

BELOW *The school in 2011.*

People of the Parish

In our first book we wrote about some of Alderbury's families and interesting individuals. More has come to light on the Fry family and Roy Pitman. Also there was a notable omission, the Fort family.

The Fort family

Members of this family owned Alderbury House and, with Lord Radnor, were the principal landowners in Alderbury. The magnificent chest tomb just outside the door of the church contains many of their names and was considered so important that it has 'listed building' status. Confusingly the eldest son was always named George. The family tree line of descent (as far as it is known at present) is shown here.

The family is reputed to have acquired by marriage in 1620, the property in Alderbury. Later, they bought up the surrounding land. In a manorial survey of 1765 George Fort (1715-90) is shown as owning and occupying 140 acres

George Fort (? - 1705)

George Fort (1684 - ?)

George Fort (1715 - 90)

George Yalden Fort (1754 - 1807)

George Fort (1784 - 1865)

George Munkhouse Fort (1815 - 1901)

George Hounsom Fort (1848 - 1917)

Edward Monkhouse Fort (1859 - 1937)

George Yalden Fort (1893 - 1963)

including a house on or near the site of the present day Alderbury House.

According to a trade directory of 1783 George Fort & Son were described as Merchants and Hat Manufacturers of Salisbury. It is known that at some stage the Fort family occupied William Russell's House, the mediaeval hall house in Queen Street, Salisbury (until recently occupied by Watsons the china and glass shop). In 1789 George Fort became Mayor of Salisbury.

In 1793 George Fort's son, George Yalden Fort (1754-1807) was an Alderman of Salisbury and in 1800 High Sheriff of Wiltshire. In 1791 he built the present Alderbury House. The family was clearly in the ascendant as in 1799 he also leased, and eventually purchased, the Manor of Winterbourne Earls with its rents.

The family took a great interest in attempts to build a local canal and George Fort (1715-90) was the instigator of a failed project in 1770. Subsequently his son George Yalden Fort (1754-1807) became a major shareholder and joint treasurer of the ill-fated Salisbury & Southampton Canal, which was started in 1795 and abandoned in 1808. The canal ran across the grounds of Alderbury House and was widened in front of the house to form a lake (which remains today), the lake also acting as one of the reservoirs for the canal.

George Fort (1784-1865) similarly invested in the local turnpike trust, the Sarum

& Eling Turnpike Trust, and in 1840 was elected Chairman of the Trustees.

In the somewhat flowery phrases of the book 'Wiltshire Leaders – Social & Political' published in 1904 *'George Hounsome Fort JP (1848-1917) received a commission in the 45th Regiment of Foot from which he retired with the rank of Captain in order to devote himself to his duties as a landowner. He is a popular landlord, a good sportsman and an active member of the County Bench'* He died childless and the estate passed to his brother Edward Munkhouse Fort (1859-1937) and in turn to Edward's son George Yalden Fort (1893-1963). On his death in 1963, Alderbury House was sold and went out of the possession of the family who had resided there for nearly 350 years. Their name lives on as Alderbury Farm in Witherington Road is still referred to locally as Fort's Farm.

However, there is an unsolved mystery regarding this family. In the Salisbury & South Wiltshire Museum there is a life-size painting of 'Miss Fort of Alderbury House' by George Beare in 1747. She is shown holding a sprig of jasmine, which may suggest that she was painted on the occasion of her marriage. Nothing is known, at present, of this young lady but it would seem that she could be a sister of George Fort (1715-90).

The Fry Family and the Salvation Army

Most people nowadays associate brass bands with the Salvation Army. The general population holds its members in high regard. It was not always like this. Churches and chapels had music but the masses had turned away from these – music and all. William Booth, the

ABOVE *Miss Fort of Alderbury House by George Beare 1747.*

founder of the Salvation Army, was not particularly musical and was inclined initially not to favour music for religious purposes. What changed his mind?

Charles William Fry was born in Alderbury in 1838, son of Abraham Fry, a journeyman bricklayer. Converted at the age of 17 in a Sunday evening prayer meeting at Alderbury's Wesleyan chapel, he soon became a local preacher. He played the violin, cello, piano and harmonium, led a small orchestra at the chapel and formed a brass band there for special occasions. He also played solo cornet in a local volunteer military band. He worked as a bricklayer and later established his own business in Salisbury as a builder.

In 1878 the Salvation Army (or Christian Mission as it was then called) started to hold meetings in Salisbury and, as had

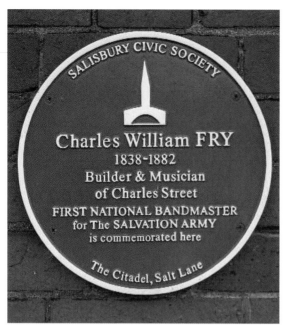

ABOVE *The plaque in Salt Lane, Salisbury.*

'Come Thou Burning Spirit Come'. He died in 1880 and is commemorated by a plaque in the cloisters of Salisbury Cathedral and in Salt Lane, Salisbury.

Meanwhile the Salvationists in Salisbury, as elsewhere, were still encountering fierce opposition at their open-air meetings and on the march and they often feared for their lives. Stones were thrown at them and sometimes things that were softer and more offensive perhaps! One hostile citizen pelted them with eggs and then went into a shop to purchase some fresh ammunition. Kicks on the shins, head wounds and black eyes were often sustained by these brave men and women. So serious did the persecution become that 50 special constables were sworn in and they marched side by side with the Salvationists. Once the Mayor accompanied them, carrying in his hand a copy of the Riot Act. At one time a society was formed *'To Stop the Parading of the Streets by the Salvation Army'* and posters appeared in Salisbury on hoardings and in shop windows. In 1886 City Council tried, unsuccessfully, to introduce a bye-law to prohibit the playing of musical instruments in Salisbury's streets. Gradually public opinion towards the Army became friendlier and in 1897 the band took part in Salisbury's celebrations of Queen Victoria's Diamond Jubilee and was invited to play at the opening of the Victoria Park.

Of Charles Fry's three sons the eldest, Frederick William Fry, also went on to achieve fame in the Salvation Army. He was born in Alderbury in 1859 and as a boy he played a cornet in the Wesleyan chapel orchestra there. By the age of eight he played the harmonium. He worked with his father in the building trade. He helped form the Army's band with his father

happened elsewhere, its members were attacked by mobs as they preached in the marketplace. Charles Fry and his three sons, sympathising with them, went to their aid and linked up with the movement. The four Frys all played brass instruments and soon the quartet was standing in Salisbury marketplace, accompanying the singing and thus the Salvation Army's first band was born.

It was soon brought to the attention of the Army's founder William Booth and he visited Salisbury to assess this innovation. He recognised the value that bands could be to the Salvation Army and eventually the decision was taken to use brass bands to attract people to the meetings. Charles Fry was appointed the Army's first bandmaster and moved to London with his family. He toured the country with the band. He wrote a number of hymns of which the most famous are 'I've Found a Friend in Jesus' and

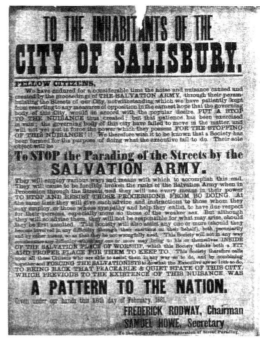

TOP LEFT *The Fry family brass band.*

ABOVE *A poster objectiong to the Salvation Army parading the streets of Salisbury.*

LEFT *The Fry family with string instruments.*

and brothers in 1878 and toured Britain extensively with them until his father died. He held a number of musical appointments at the Army's headquarters and was, for a while, William Booth's private secretary. In 1891 he was appointed Bandmaster of the movement's International Staff Band. Like his father, he wrote a number of hymns.

Roy Pitman:
a Naturalist at Home

In his obituary of Roy Pitman (1905-86) Ralph Whitlock, himself a noted author and broadcaster, compared him to the great pioneer naturalists Gilbert White, Richard Jefferies and W. H. Hudson. Roy was an all-round naturalist of the old school with nothing being beyond his interest, although his especial interest was entomology. He is probably best remembered for his book A Naturalist at Home and for his work on the BBC's World in Action television programme The Petersfinger Cuckoos. He also edited the Wiltshire Bird Report for the Wiltshire Archaeological and Natural History Magazine for a time. In 1936, he was appointed the official recorder of insect immigration for Wiltshire by the Society for British Entomology. He contributed nature notes to the Salisbury Journal and The Fountain and appeared in Kite's Country on television. He is reputed to have been, along with Major Oliver Kite, the presenter of the programme, the last person to have crossed the River Avon using the punt at Ferry Cottage (and it is said to have leaked like a sieve).

He was, however, just as happy passing on his knowledge of, and passion for, nature to anyone who wished to ask. Indeed, only a couple of months or so before his death he was pictured in the Avon Advertiser showing some of his collection to youngsters in Salisbury Library and identifying insects and other creatures the children had brought in. He was constantly brought strange creatures to identify, or save, by all sorts of people. One of our members can remember accompanying him to look at the remains of the old walnut tree which used to stand on The Green. There he was looking for stag beetles which were nesting in the rotten tree stump and which, even at that time (in the 1980s), were growing increasingly rare. He would walk for miles and had the rare ability to spot things which no-one else would give a second glance and was more often than not able to identify them immediately.

His home was initially in Rampart Road in Salisbury. In April 1938 he moved to a 'house in the country', believed to be 'Malvern' in what is now Marshmead Close at Clarendon but which then fronted on to the main Salisbury to Southampton Road. However, as it backed on to fields and the river, the house was in an ideal spot to indulge his hobby. Later (probably in the 1970s) he moved to 'Karushel' in Southampton Road, Whaddon, which again backed on to fields. His working life began as a gardener, possibly to indulge the passion for nature which he had acquired as a small boy. In the late 1920s he was assistant curator at Salisbury and South Wilts Museum, which was then situated in St Ann Street, and in the middle of the next decade founded, along with Ralph Whitlock, the Field Club. This seems to have foundered at some later date - quite possibly with the onset of war. In 1952 it was re-founded as the Salisbury & District Natural History Society. He remained a vice-president of the society until his death.

During the Second World War he served as a special constable and even then managed to combine his studies of the natural world with his official duties, describing in his book how he observed *a desperate struggle between a cock salmon and an otter in the River Avon alongside the solicitors' chambers in Bridge Street, Salisbury*. In later years he worked at the Microbiological Department at Porton Down.

At the time of his death he was sorting notes for a companion volume to A Naturalist at Home but unfortunately this task was never completed.

Although nature was his passion it wasn't his only interest - he was a fine village cricketer and when his playing days were over, took up umpiring instead. He also donated a Married v Singles Cup which was played for by teams from within the club for several years. Roy was also a keen angler and was vice-president of the Salisbury & District Angling Club for many years.

LEFT *Roy Pitman, noted author and broadcaster.*

Earning a Living

The earliest mention of people's employment in Alderbury comes from the 1379 Poll Tax returns when 17 residents were described as tilers. They were, of course, tile-makers manufacturing tiles for the royal palaces at Clarendon and Ludgershall, as well as for the public buildings and private residences in Salisbury and the surrounding area. In the city's accounts there is a reference in 1436 of a payment to *John Spencer of Alwardbury for the tiling'* (of the almshouse).

RIGHT

Blacksmith

Edward

Langridge's

will

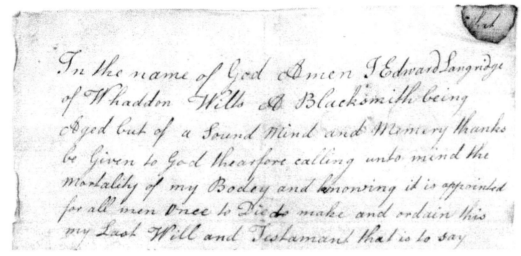

Blacksmiths and Wheelwrights

There were smithies at both Alderbury and Whaddon. Sometimes besides the master blacksmith there would be a journeyman blacksmith (a qualified assistant who had served a long apprenticeship) and possibly one or more apprentices. Besides shoeing horses and making and repairing ploughs, the smith would have made and sold a wide range of tools and implements. We know from their wills the names of some of the earliest blacksmiths. For example, in 1671 John Dennis blacksmith of Alderbury left goods totalling £52.16s.9d. (approximately £4,000 in today's values). Similarly, in 1696 John Harris of Alderbury left £94.9s.7d. (approx. £7,000), while in 1718

Thomas Tanner of Whaddon left £131.7s.0d (over £10,000). According to the inventory his goods included a cow and hay worth £2! Other wills were for George Tutt of Alderbury in 1803 and Edward Langridge of Whaddon in 1815. William Dowty was Alderbury's longest serving blacksmith with over 40 years from the 1830s. John Mouland followed him for 30 years from 1885 with James Sims followed by Charles Worsdell until 1939. Then came father and son, Stanley and Peter Riches, and latterly Basil Elliott.

The master wheelwright held a similar place to the blacksmith in the hierarchy of the village in that he would probably employ several carpenters and joiners. The making of bodies and underframes for the large four-wheeled wagons was their task, while the manufacture of iron-tyred wooden wheels required the specialist skills of the wheelwright. Again, we know from their wills the names of some of the earliest wheelwrights. In 1682 Richard Miles of Whaddon left £130.4s.0d. (over £10,000). Edward Spragg and his son, also Edward, both of Alderbury, left wills in 1751 and 1793 respectively. We also know they employed apprentices, John Elphs of Downton in 1716 and William Flander in 1755.

Mantua-maker and Cordwainer

Two occupations not met with in the present day are mantua-maker and cordwainer. A mantua-maker was what we now call a dressmaker. In 1730 Mary Hill, mantua-maker of Alderbury, took an apprentice for four years, Frances King of Dean. A cordwainer was a worker in leather – anything from leather bottles and shoes to horse harnesses. The term was most commonly used of shoemakers. In 1753 John Gauntlet, cordwainer of Whaddon, took an apprentice, Aaron Wiltshire. Some members of the Dowty family were shoemakers in the 19th century.

Tailors and Butchers

In his novel 'Martin Chuzzlewit', published in 1843-4, Charles Dickens immortalised the bandy-legged tailor leaving the Blue Dragon and he has been identified as William Lewis from a family of tailors of that name who lived in Alderbury at that time. Other members of the Lewis family were sub-postmasters. The History Group has written about sub-postmasters in a separate publication on Alderbury's post office.

Butchers who left wills were Thomas Moody (1731) and Robert Moody (1754). The latter also described himself as a yeoman. Similarly in the 1840s William Beaumont described himself as both butcher and innkeeper – he probably used one of his rooms as an alehouse in his cottage on the corner of Old Road and Clarendon Road, now Cherry Tree Cottage. Innkeepers and alehouse-keepers are also fully dealt with in a separate publication by the History Group.

Farmers and Farm Labourers

Besides the Longford and Clarendon estates, farmers were major employers of labour in the village with over half the adult male population being agricultural labourers. People who research their family history nowadays will recognise the abbreviation 'Ag. Lab.' beloved of census-takers. Thanks to the Tithe Award and censuses we are able to reconstruct the farms and farmers in the mid-nineteenth century. The largest farm at 570 acres was Matrons' College Farm. It was farmed by Stephen Parsons who employed 28 labourers. This farm has also been known variously as Charity Farm, Tozer's Farm and, confusingly, Whaddon Farm. It was, and is, owned by Bishop Seth Ward's Charity, the rent going to support the almshouse for poor clergy widows, known as Matrons' College, which is situated just inside the High Street Gate of Salisbury Cathedral Close.

Nearby Whaddon Farm, which was situated opposite the Three Crowns, was 236 acres, being owned by the Longford Estate and farmed by Mark Phillips, who employed 19

labourers. The Longford Estate also owned Rectory Farm, at the end of Rectory Road, and George Rumbold, who employed 3 labourers, farmed its 78 acres. Not surprisingly the lane in which Rectory Farm stands was then known as Rumbold's Lane.

George Fort owned Alderbury Farm of 312 acres, along Standlynch Road (now Witherington Road) and he employed a bailiff to farm it. Shoot End Farm on Lower Road was then by the present-day entrance to Alward House. It was about 40 acres and was owned by the Longford Estate. In 1851 it was farmed by Ambrose Phillips and subsequently by Mark Light, employing 3 men and 2 boys. In 1890 his son-in-law Robert Taylor had taken over the dairy farm. With the building of Alward House in 1903, the Taylors' dairy farm moved to the

ABOVE *Fred Down of Spiders Island, forking mangolds on T. Tozer's farm (Matron's College Farm) March 1935.*

ABOVE *Men stacking hay with Len Bowden by his tractor.*

top of Silver Street, retaining its name for the farmhouse. This family ran their dairy business in Salisbury and the surrounding villages until 1975. Some villagers will remember Fred Taylor who eventually ran the milk delivery leaving his brothers to run the farming side of the business.

Building firms

Another long-running business was the Eyres family of wheelwrights, carpenters and builders who occupied Wisteria Cottage at the top of Silver Street with the carpenter's shop in the large shed there. This had previously been occupied by the Prewett family of wheelwrights and carpenters. Eyres and Sons, as is so often the case in villages, besides making coffins, also acted as undertakers. Albert Eyres and his two sons, William and Albert built the pair of semi-detached houses named Chuzzlewit and Doward on Southampton Road at the top of Silver Street. The sons occupied these houses and the yard behind them was also used for the family business. After World War I they realised that with the advent of the motor car their traditional business of wheelwright was in decline and they extended their carpentry business into house building. In total they built about 20 houses in Alderbury, ranging from small bungalows in Firs Road to Redlands in Southampton Road built in 1939 for Mr and Mrs Austin Parsons.

Another firm of builders, who built mainly in Whaddon, was F. Hand & Sons. They had extended their business from making bricks and extracting sand, into building houses. The Whaddon Brickworks was founded in about 1904, on land leased from Matrons'

College Farm, by the Hand family who owned it until its closure in 1976. The bypass now covers much of the site; the entrance was on the eastern side of Southampton Road just past the Post office and the former railway bridge. In 1925 Walter Tanner was listed as the manager with at least nine other employees. The family tradition continued with Ralph Tanner who was the brickmaker in 1962. He lived in Crossfields Cottage, at the far end of Rectory Road, and is remembered by older residents in the area who visited the works and helped out at busy times on a voluntary basis. The local handmade bricks can still be seen in many village properties. The full story of brick and tilemaking in Alderbury and Whaddon can be found in one of the History Group's other publications.

Sand and Gravel Extraction

As anyone who has tried to grow roses in many parts of the village will testify, the subsoil here is largely sand or gravel. Writing in 1685 in his Natural History of Wiltshire, John Aubrey stated *'At Alderbury, by Ivy Church, is great plenty of fine gravelle which is sent for all over the south parts of the country.'* It is some time since gravel was extracted here, but older residents will recall the gravel pit behind The Old Post Office Cottage in Old Road, which was eventually used for landfill. The 1809 Enclosure Award referred to two gravel pits in Alderbury. The accompanying map showed a small lane in the area of Old Chapel Close naming it as Gravel Pit Lane. According to the 1847 Tithe Map the field between there and Lights Lane was known as Great Gravel Pit. There was also a gravel pit on the site of Silver Wood and another behind the yard at Home Farm.

There have been many sites around the village which have been sandpits until they were largely worked out. In 1875, 59 acres at Whaddon were put up for sale and the sale particulars mentioned *'it contains an unlimited supply of white and yellow sand of fine quality and great value'.* The accompanying map showed that this was land bordered by Grimstead Road, Southampton Road and the canal. It included the current site of Pepperbox Rise, Spiders Island and the Avon Drive estate. In 1931 the Pepperbox Rise site was a sandpit owned by the Longford Estate and let to the Hand family firm. From 1935 to 1942 it was let to Boswell Brothers of Ford. It was not worked out but was requisitioned by the Army in 1944.

There were two other less well-known sites at that time. One was in Rectory Road. A valuation of a Sand Mine (sic) there in 1932-3 for Sidney Burton stated the site was worked out and that it was proposed to 'level up the swamp'. It subsequently became a poultry farm. Similarly, a valuation of a sandpit for Alfred Williams at Heatherfield in Lights Lane (a property previously known as Sandhills) showed that it had been worked from 1929-35 when the pit was exhausted. It was filled in and sold as a poultry farm. The sand had consisted of a seam 16 inches deep.

The most famous sandpit, of course, is that now occupied by the housing estate The Sandringhams. Again the Hand family worked this. A member of that family told how his grandfather, Frederick Hand, *'used to work the sandpit with an employee and they had a 100-ft. face of sand. Their habit was to dig a cave at the bottom and then they got the sand to fall down as this method saved them two days work. In*

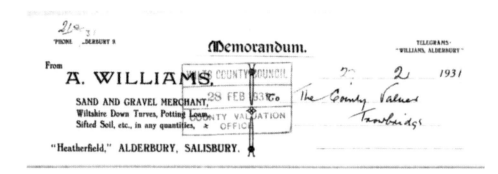

LEFT *Alfred Williams at Heatherfield in Lights Lane where the sandpit was worked from 1929-35.*

November 1944 they were doing this but hadn't realised that a hard frost the night before had loosened the sand and it collapsed on them. The employee managed to run but was caught in loose sand up to his knees. However he managed to escape and phone the rest of the family. They came and dug but it wasn't until the afternoon that they found the dead body of grandfather. When they found him he was still standing with his shovel in his hand'.

No Health & Safety regulations in those days!

Motor Engineers

What is now (in 2011) M & M Auto Engineers, next to Hurstbourne House, began in the 1930s as Hand's Garage, originally intended to service and repair the steam engines operating in the nearby sandpits. This was not the first garage in the village. The first garage replaced the forge at Whaddon, run by blacksmith James Moody. This business was owned by the Enright Brothers who were described in the local directory for 1925 as motor mechanics at The Green at Whaddon. By 1927 it was known as Bridge Garage being adjacent to the bridge that carried the railway over the road; it was operated by Austin Parsons. In 1956 it was sold to Anna Valley Motors who operated it for only a short while.

Meanwhile Charles Robinson (affectionately known locally as Charlie Robinson) had, during World War II, bought Hurstbourne House and the neighbouring garage from the Hand family and started in business there after the war. He had installed petrol pumps even when petrol was still rationed. In the 1950s he also bought from the Longford Estate the disused sandpit immediately across the road. He built a new workshop and showroom and moved the petrol pumps there. Then he bought the Bridge Motors site from Anna Valley Motors, knocking down a dilapidated workshop and built a small kiosk to serve the petrol pumps there. In 1964 he sold out his whole operation to Matthew McQueen & Co. Ltd. In 1972 the main site had been bought by Yeates Coaches and in 1993

ABOVE *Robinson's garage, now Pepperbox Rise estate.*

sold for building development now the Pepperbox Rise estate. The original site continued as Hurstbourne Garage, motor body builders, but at present it is not known when they ceased trading. It remained unoccupied for a number of years until 1995 when M & M Auto Engineers acquired it. They are VW and Audi specialists but also service and repair all makes of car.

Meanwhile in the early 1970s Bridge Garage had been occupied by Securicor Ltd. and subsequently by DKB Industries, which originally did some car servicing, as well as their lawnmower sales and servicing. The wheel has turned full circle as the site has been acquired by M & M Auto Engineers who hope to sell their old site for housing and build a new garage on the Bridge Garage site.

Near the Green Dragon, 4x4 Services who have been operating there since 1985 have been taken over by Brooklyn 4x4 Services of Nursling, a company with whom they have been working closely for the past six years. They now occupy only the building on the right-hand of that site. The left-hand building is now occupied by Alderbury Garage, formerly Grimstead Garage run for the past 12 years by Jonathan West at Duckpond Lane, East Grimstead. Andy Riches, Alderbury Garage's MOT tester, is no stranger as he grew up in Forge Cottage opposite.

Shops and Shopkeepers

The pubs and post office have been covered in separate publications by the History Group but mention should be made of the village shops. At Whaddon the censuses 1851-81 list George Light as a grocer and it is probable that it was situated at Tetherings, off Castle Lane, as he is shown as owning it in the 1847 Tithe Award, although he does not appear to be resident at that time. By the 1890s the shop was at its present location on Southampton Road with John Angel listed in the local directory as the shopkeeper in 1897 and from 1898 his wife Fanny Angel. In 1904 it was run by the interestingly named Urban Bray. By 1912 the familiar name of William Occomore was shown as baker and grocer, followed in the 1930s by his son Reginald Occomore when the shop was known as Bridge Stores. In 1972 Alan Griggs took over and many will remember him for his long distance cycling exploits and in particular his 'Beaujolais Run' for the new season's wine. With the taking down of the bridge the name was changed to Post Office Stores. He was followed by David and Lesley Aylott and most recently by Jason Holden.

Throughout most of the latter half of the 1800s, at the top of Silver Street in what is now Shute End Farmhouse, was the shop of William Waterman, grocer and baker. He was followed by Arthur Lewis, who also held the sub-postmaster's job for a while in the 1890s and early 1900s. The Lewis family also had the shop at the end of the High Street in the person of William Lewis in the 1850s and James Lewis in the 1860s and they combined it with selling beer. James was also described as a brewer and it is during his occupancy that mention is first made of the premises next to the shop being described as the Goose Inn. The 1870s saw

BELOW

*Hickman's
Stores, now
High Street.*

HICKMAN'S STORES, ALDERBURY.

Newton Bungay there, having returned from Australia after a spell in the goldfields. From the 1880s to the 1930s the name of William Hickman appears and although there is no mention of beer retailing, it became a bakery as well as grocery. From the 1930s to 1950s B. E. Viney was grocer there. Then it was bought by the Salisbury Co-operative Society and remained in their ownership until it closed in the 1970s.

The Alderbury Shop in Canal Lane was originally started by Mr Edwards for three mornings a week in his front room at 'Verona', Southampton Road; many will remember Ralph and Molly Galpin and Roger Chalk before the present owner known by everyone as 'Warren'. Older residents will remember the butcher's shop on the corner of Castle Lane, opposite the old police station, owned by William Newell 1931-66. Then F.G.Catterall owned it. From 1968-71 it was owned by G. W. Yearling, after which it ceased trading.

A Travel Agent

Right next door to the Green Dragon in the converted barn is one of Alderbury's best kept secrets. Not many people in the village know that Andante Travel is owned and run by archaeologists, providing archaeological and historical holidays throughout the world. The Council for British Archaeology has commended them as the leading tour operator in this specialised field. They are particularly proud of the fact that their Guide Lecturers are frequently closely associated with the archaeological scene in the specific area of the ancient world being visited.

Smallholders

During the 1920s and 1930s there were a great number of smallholdings, some being poultry farmers and others market gardeners. Some names from that period: Leonard Bowden in Silver Street, Richard Bundy at Southampton Road, Sidney Burton in Rectory Road, Miss Caroline Cloud at 'Richmond', Southampton Road, Albert England at Whaddon, Sidney Hatcher at Ladies Cottages, Mark Newell at Clarendon Road, Harry Poole in what is now Canal Lane, George Rose at Ivychurch, Edward Thorne at Clarendon Road, Charles Vincent at Southampton Road and Reginald Witt at Whaddon. Their activities are an area of ongoing research for the History Group and we would be pleased to hear from anyone with more information to the limited amount that we already hold. One interesting snippet: in 1949 Harry Poole bought the first chicken plucking machine in the area and farmers brought their chickens to be plucked for market.

Whaddon Business Park

The building of the Whaddon Business Park in 1989 besides ensuring the continued existence of the post office and shop and the Three Crowns, also brought with it a new opportunity for local employment. Apart from those who work there, not many people are aware of these businesses and what they do.

Halyard Marine

To win the Queen's Award for Industry is rare. To win it twice is exceptional. Whaddon's largest employer has done just that. The company designs and manufactures exhaust silencing systems and vibration control products for marine engines. It employs 75 staff and has three manufacturing sites, two in Portsmouth and one in Ferndown, as well as its design centre and headquarters at Whaddon. It won its first Queen's Award in 2006 for innovation in meeting European noise regulations and its second in 2010 for demonstrating a process of continuous innovation.

Embroidery Unlimited

Rosalind Gray, of the well known Alderbury family of that name, has the distinction of having grown her own business over the last 20 years; she moved to the business park in 2000. Her company, of which Ros is the sole director, is an embroidery and monogram specialist supplying principally embroidery and printed clothing. Many in the village will remember the mug supplied by them to commemorate the Millennium.

Inn Gear

This company is the UK's largest supplier of artwork, artefacts and themed bric-a-brac to the brewery, restaurant and hotel industries. An example of their work can be seen in Whaddon's Three Crowns where, during the refurbishment, Inn Gear asked for the History Group's co-operation in supplying local postcards which they enlarged and framed, providing interesting talking points for customers.

Trekwear

This company is an Internet supplier of skiwear, outdoor clothing, waterproof jackets, walking boots, rucksacks and much more. Founded in 2007 by Managing Director Robin Longworth at Gardners Farm in Plaitford, they moved to Whaddon in 2008.

Freelance Entry Solutions Ltd

Supplying and installing all the leading makes of garage doors since 1994 was this company's speciality. More recently they decided to enlarge their sphere of operations into property protection products such as security shutters, retractable gates and grilles, anti-vandal glazing screens and anti-climb bars, both for residential and commercial applications.

Gearlink Ltd

Well known for its ownership of the very successful Gearlink Kawasaki motorcycle racing team, this company is also a specialist in reconditioned gearboxes. They supply them both to private individuals and to a large established base of main-dealer trade customers.

Images at Work Ltd

Formed in 1989 this company has become one of the UK's leaders in the field of corporate clothing management. Recently they were awarded contracts with police and fire services to provide a fully managed supply and after-care package for all uniform and personal protection equipment garments. They are particularly proud to have been involved over four years in assisting the British Steam Car Team secure five land-speed records in 2009. Initially they supplied the team uniform and their merchandise. Subsequently they were instrumental in the creation of protective clothing for the support crew, very necessary as they were at risk from high-pressure steam and

heat, with the car churning out up to 400 degrees Celsius.

Spire Glass

In Whaddon since 1989, this company provides a wide range of glass and glazing solutions, including casement windows, tilt and turn, aluminium, glazing to wood, conservatories and other high-specification architectural glazing, such as patent glazing and mirrors.

Moleroda Finishing Systems Ltd

The latest addition to the business park, this company has moved in 2011 from March Farm in Farley. It is the UK's largest felt and specialist polishing accessory manufacturer, exporting to over 20 countries worldwide. Their manufacturing expertise includes polishing in felt, diamond, wood, calicos, fine abrasive cloths, unitised material and abrasive non-woven nylon.

Oakridge Office Park

The new office park at Whaddon with its landmark clock tower has attracted not only a number of small firms but also a firm of solicitors who have become famous nationally and internationally.

William Bache & Co. Solicitors

They were founded in Salisbury in 2005 as a niche practice to deal principally with parents and carers of children wrongly accused of harming their children, dealing with criminal and family courts. The principal William (Bill) Bache has spent over 30 years in the law, the majority of that time as a partner in a Salisbury practice, specialising in criminal work, child care and courts martial matters. Mr Bache's profile was raised both nationally and internationally when he was asked to represent Angela Cannings, a Salisbury mother who was accused of murdering two of her children. That case went on to become the catalyst which instigated the biggest shake up in English Law for many years and resulted in many similar cases being reviewed by the Attorney General.

ML Electronics

This company is the latest occupier of the office park having expanded its operations from Brickworth Lane in Whiteparish to open a second office at Whaddon. They provide innovative electronic product design and development solutions, right through from creative design to their in-house manufacturing capability. An impressive client list includes Alcan, Amstrad, Ferrari and Qinetiq.

ABOVE *The clock tower on the Oakridge offices at Whaddon.*

Other Occupations and Companies

Reasons of space have prevented us from including a completely comprehensive list of companies and it has been made more difficult by those who, in this day of the computer, work from home. However we have one unique self-employed individual in Alderbury whom we felt we could not omit.

Jonathan the Jester

Salisbury's official City Jester, an unpaid role, has won many plaudits including European Jester of the Year 1999. In 2006 he broke the world record for the longest ever street-show performing for 26 hours in Salisbury Market Place. His performance includes juggling, low-level tightropes, globe and unicycling, as well as the usual clowning around. Besides making a living at his unusual job, he has also helped raise many thousands of pounds for charity.

99

Random Gleanings

All historians gather bits and pieces of historical information that they hope will one day fit into a larger picture. Here are some of the more interesting items filling in a few of the gaps of our mosaic.

Smuggling

Most of us associate smuggling with groups of men unloading contraband at night from small boats, possibly with bloody clashes with the excisemen. But what happened to the smuggled goods after that? In Kipling's words:

'Five and twenty ponies, Trotting through the dark - Brandy for the Parson, 'Baccy for the Clerk'.

On the nights following the landing, strings of ponies would take the goods using quiet tracks, to inland distribution centres such as Salisbury. One such route from the coast would have followed the valley of the River Avon passing through Alderbury. The Salisbury & Winchester Journal of 8 January 1787 records *'200 barrels of brandy were hidden in a coppice at Alderbury and seized by the excisemen on Christmas Day'*. We shall never know whether Alderbury's parson would have been the recipient of any of that brandy!

Robbery and Attempted Murder

The Salisbury & Winchester Journal for 14 November 1796 tells the story of a dastardly deed on Alderbury Common:

'On Wednesday evening last, about half past six o'clock, as a gardener was coming from Dean, in a cart, to this city, he was stopped at the gate on Alderbury Common, leading to Grimstead, by two men in soldier's cloaths, who robbed him of a trifling sum of money, all that he had about

him, and afterwards brutally cut and stabbed him on the head with a bayonet, and knocked him from the cart, merely because he had no more to give them. A person of Alderbury hastened up on hearing his cries, and the villains then made off into a wood. It is thought they intended to murder the poor man, and would have effected their purpose, had not the bayonet been broken at the point, as clearly appears by the wound on his skull. – Two soldiers of the 58th Regiment of Foot were seen in the neighbourhood about the time of the robbery, and from some circumstances are suspected to have perpetrated it; but they have not yet been traced, nor has any other discovery been made, likely to tend to a detection of the villains'.

A fascinating aftermath to the story was that almost 200 years later that very same bayonet (identical down to the broken tip) was found while digging his garden at the end of Clarendon Road by the late Brian Burton - about a hundred yards from the scene of the crime! It is now in the possession of the History Group.

Marconi and His Experiment from Pepperbox Hill

The sending of the first wireless message across the Atlantic in 1901 by the Italian, Guglielmo

Marconi is common knowledge. Less widely known is that five years before, in 1896, Marconi conducted an experiment from Pepperbox Hill, sending a signal four miles. Radio Alderbury!

More Vicars

Although the Treasurers of the Cathedral were responsible for appointing vicars to Alderbury Church, their records are incomplete, as is the listing in the church, which was compiled from various sources. A recent discovery at the Wiltshire & Swindon Record Office of a will dated 1567 for Richard Leveridge, Vicar of Alderbury, indicates that he should be added to the list. Similarly it is now known that John Crouch, shown on that list for 1661, was appointed in 1657 and ejected in 1662 after being charged at the Quarter Sessions for not reading Common Prayer. He was clearly a Presbyterian Minister appointed during the Interregnum and following the restoration of Charles II he was ejected from office. It is known that he subsequently preached in Salisbury, Allington and Newton Tony and afterwards in London as a Congregational Minister. Also to be added to the list is Edward Hillary 1655-6. He was almost certainly an Anglican, as in 1657 he became Rector of Compton Beauchamp in Berkshire.

Windmills

Both Alderbury and Whaddon had windmills. Very little is known about the one at Alderbury, other than that it stood in the field on the corner of Old Road and Clarendon Road. The field was known as Windmill Close. The latest record known of this mill was in Greenwood's map of 1820.

For Whaddon Mill, the story starts in 1798 when the Earl of Ilchester granted to John Roberts, a miller of West Harnham, a 99-year lease of one acre on Whaddon Common *'subject to John Roberts erecting within 12 months a Wind Grist Mill'*. He erected the mill and in 1799 mortgaged it to Isaac White, a baker of New Sarum.

By 1800 it was advertised for sale in the Salisbury & Winchester Journal: *'To be sold by private contract, all that newly erected windmill, called Whaddon Mill now in complete repair, situate on Whaddon Common, nr. Salisbury, Wilts; together with an acre of land thereto adjoining, and of which immediate possession will be given'*. Ownership of the premises was transferred by Roberts and White to Edward Dunham, a wheelwright from Fareham. He in turn sold it to Robert Head a landowner of Whaddon. Eventually the Head family sold it in 1822 to the Earl of Radnor.

There are two mentions of the tenants of the mill. The first in The London Gazette for 1806 stated that *'Abraham Golding, late of Alderbury, miller, a prisoner for debt in Fisherton Anger gaol'*. The second was in the Poor Rate Book for Alderbury in 1827 when Charles Stanford was listed as occupier. No other references to the mill have been found since that date. So where was the Whaddon Mill? It was in the area of the Avon Drive and Spiders Island estates – almost certainly at the highest point.

Village Orchestra

A hundred years ago Alderbury had a village orchestra. A report in the Salisbury Journal in 1909 recorded that they gave a concert in the schoolroom in aid of the Salisbury Infirmary.

The History Group would like to know whether anyone has more information about the orchestra.

We Now Know

It happens to all historians, both amateur and professional, that new information comes to light which changes earlier published views or interpretations.

It had been thought that the coach house at the Green Dragon in Alderbury was the location of the first meeting of the Methodists in the Salisbury area. We now know that there was also an inn of that name in Fisherton Street, Salisbury whose coach house was the true location.

Coaches Through Alderbury

In the days of horse-drawn traffic a number of coaches would have passed through Alderbury and Whaddon en route from or to Salisbury. Perhaps the most famous of these would have been the Red Rover travelling between Bristol and Southampton, calling at The Antelope in Catherine Street, Salisbury. This coach has given its name to the Red Rover pub at West Wellow.

As befitting a coach carrying the Royal Mail, precise times of departure and arrival were published for the coach to Portsmouth from Salisbury. *'Mail from the Black Horse Hotel, leaves half past one at night, arrives half past twelve at night, daily through Romsey, Southampton (Royal Hotel), Fareham and Cosham.'* Similarly precise was the packet from The Lamb at Salisbury to Southampton, *'Leaving at 9 in the morning and returns daily at 8'*. The most frequent coaches were those for Southampton and the Isle of Wight *'Coaches to and from the Black Horse Hotel ten times a day'*.

Poorer people would have travelled on the long distance carriers cart (a covered wagon) of which there was one to Portsmouth, three to Southampton, two to both Southampton and Portsmouth and one to Romsey and Southampton.

Whaddon Church: Its Fate

Like the churches at Farley and Pitton, Whaddon Church was originally a dependent chapel to the Minster church of Alderbury. Subsequently it became a dependent chapel of Ivychurch Priory. To cut a long story short, eventually it was abandoned and fell into disrepair. In 1815 the Vicar of Alderbury stated *'vestiges remained until lately'*.

So where was Whaddon Church? A member of the Hand family told the History Group that during the early 1940s his grandfather, while working the sandpit at the site of what is now The Sandringhams estate, had come across what he thought were the foundations of the church. He did not report it as *'he did not want to be held up by the archaeologists'*. It is certainly a likely site as originally it would have been a small hill. Some dressed stones have found their way to various gardens in Whaddon!

Challenge To A Boxing Match

In the Salisbury & Winchester Journal for 1768 there is a fascinating correspondence: Thomas Brown of Tytherly complains of the *'spiteful, ill-natured, brutish Fellow'* who put on a lock and chain to prevent him returning through the Gate at Sherill *'if he has any manly behaviour'*, asks him to name and place, and desires to box him for 5 or 10 guineas, and to bring his second with him. The following week's edition brings a response to the challenger that he will meet him at the Green Dragon Inn at Alderbury on Wednesday at 2.00, with his second and the money – he predicts *'the Brown shall be sent home Black'*.

Frustratingly, there the tale ends with no indication of the result!

REVISED RULES

OF THE

ALDERBURY, WHADDON AND PETERSFINGER
PIG CLUB.

1.—Each Member joining the Club to pay 1/- Entrance Fee, and 6d. per quarter Subscription to be paid in advance at each Quarterly Meeting.

2.—Each Member shall pay 1/- per Pig for Insurance on entering same. *See rules 4 & 11*

3.—Any Member not Paying his or her Subscription on Quarter Night shall, after three months, not receive any benefit for loss, and shall cease to be a Member, and shall only be re-admitted as a new Member.

4.—Any Member on entering a Pig or Pigs shall ask Two Members of the Committee to examine them, and their decision shall be final; all Pigs should be examined within seven days after purchase, but cannot be insured unless found healthy and in a comfortable position.

Saving the Bacon

More information has come to light about this club founded in 1895 by William Hill, a house steward of the Earl of Radnor. It is not known when it ceased to function but it was in existence for more than half a century including the two world wars. Its purpose was to insure its members in the event of their pigs dying or contracting diseases. Subscriptions for members and that of their pigs, breeding sows and boars, had to be paid on entering the scheme and then quarterly, provided the animals had been examined within seven days of entry by two members of the committee and declared healthy and in a 'comfortable position'. If an insured pig died, or was ill, two appointed members would inspect and value the animal and if circumstances dictated, order it to be killed. If unfit to be used as food or in the event of compulsory slaughter due to Swine Fever, the distressed member would be compensated.

The committee consisted of 16 members including a chairman, secretary and treasurer. There was a social side to enjoy for members and non-members with an annual dinner and smoking concert in the W.I. Hut.

An Elopement

'WHEREAS Ann the Wife of Joseph Russell of the Three Crowns at Whaddon, did on Wednesday last, elope. This is to caution all persons not to trust her, as no debts she may hereafter contract will be discharged by me.

JOSEPH RUSSELL December 3, 1790'.

From the Salisbury & Winchester Journal

A Local Legend Disproved

In their book 'Clarendon: Landscape of Kings', Professor Tom Beaumont James and Christopher Gerrard write:

'There is less substance in the local legend that Edward III and his two royal prisoners, David II of Scotland and John II of France enjoyed a hunting party together at Clarendon in 1357'.

The legend suggests they stopped for refreshment at the Three Crowns at Whaddon, giving their name to the establishment. Leaving aside the question of whether there was any building on that site at the time, the authors go on to say:

'King David was almost certainly not there in that year, when the three kings were supposed to have been taking refuge from the plague in London. For one thing there is no recorded outbreak of bubonic plague in 1357, although there might have been some other disease in the capital. The story of the hunting party can be traced back only to

John Britton's account published in 1801'.

So we have to fall back on the more prosaic explanation that the Three Crowns, like all the other pubs of that name in the country, is named for the biblical Three Kings and no, we don't think they stopped at Whaddon on their way to Bethlehem!

A Careless Housewife

'On Thursday last, about one o'clock in the Afternoon, a Fire broke out in a Shepherd's House at Whaddon, near Sarum, occasioned by the carelessness of his Wife, in throwing a broom, (with which she had been sweeping her oven) on some Heather or Straw, which set Fire to the same, the Flames soon communicated itself to four other Houses, which were entirely consumed; with the greatest part of their Household Goods and Wearing Apparel, with three Barns, in which were several Loads of Wheat, and also two Hay-Ricks, and one Oat-Pick'.

Salisbury & Winchester Journal 15 August 1737

Land Girls at Longford

During World War I Wiltshire was in the forefront of the formation of the Women's Land Army set up because of a shortage of farm-workers as so many men had gone to war. Initially, five Schools for Milkers were set up including the Longford School for Milkers at Home Farm Alderbury with the girls using part of Longford Castle Estate Office as a hostel. These were so successful that subsequently their training extended to other branches of agriculture.

Lady Pembroke and Edith Olivier (later

to be Mayor of Wilton) were very involved on the War Agricultural Committee and the latter tells an amusing story:

'These Longford pupils were girls of the so-called "educated" classes, and I always met them at Salisbury station and drove them to Longford. The first time I went to meet a batch, I accosted all the most attractive-looking girls that I saw and asked if they were coming to the Dairy School. Most of them looked very much offended, and, drawing themselves up with great haughtiness, they answered: "No". I learnt my lesson, and the next time I met a train I asked the girls: "Are you coming to Longford Castle?" They always looked rather flattered at this, and if I had made a mistake they answered quite apologetically "No, not today". Then they watched with impressed faces as I led off my little band'.

And Finally

Some unusual burials from the Alderbury Registers:

1627 Andrew a Blackemoore servant to Th. Dove Esq.

1627 Elizabeth Lynch, the daughter of John Lynch, one who dyed as is supposed of ye pestilence.

1627 Cisily Froude who died of the pestilence.

1645 2 souldiers slayne at Alderbury that were of the Garrison of Langford.

1667 widow Elcock a Quaker died suddenly in the night and was buried at a place called Privalte in the p'ish of Downton by a company of Quakers w'ch said quaker had foure bastards by her maister and not known till after her death having lived in these pts above 30 yeares.

Index